The Herbace   Affair of
Cocaine Claire

The 4th Case for
Inspector Capstan

David Blake

www.david-blake.com

Edited and proofread by Lorraine Swoboda

Cover design by David Blake

Published in Great Britain, 2016

Disclaimer:
These are works of fiction. Names, characters, businesses, places, events and incidents are either the products of the author's imagination or used in a fictitious manner. Any resemblance to actual persons, living or dead, or actual events is purely coincidental.

ISBN: 1539845656
ISBN-13: 978-1539845652

DEDICATION

For Akiko, Akira and Kai.

THE INSPECTOR CAPSTAN
SERIES INCLUDES:

CONTENTS

The Herbaceous Affair of Cocaine Claire

ACKNOWLEDGMENTS

I'd like to thank my family for putting up with me and my rather odd sense of humour.

I'd also like to thank my Editor and Proofreader, Lorraine Swoboda, for making sure that what I write makes sense, sort of, and that all the words are in the right order.

Chapter One
Give a dog a bad name

Monday, 27th July
09:15 BST

WITH BOTH HANDS handcuffed in front of him, and dressed head to foot in a brand new issue of prison overalls, Portsmouth Prison's latest arrival, inmate number 3471, formerly known as Police Chief Inspector Morose of the Solent Constabulary, stood quietly in front of the Prison's Warden who'd yet to acknowledge his presence.

Engrossed in a particularly large file that lay on his desk sat the Warden himself, a Mr Oliver Obtuse, who was using one hand to turn over the pages and the other to eat a toasted bacon and egg sandwich.

Every now and again he'd stop to stare down at one of the many black and white photographs contained within the file, each of which featured a similar picture of a severed head with matching pairs of hands and feet, before swallowing the contents of his mouth to begin tutting loudly, and rather obviously. He'd then take another bite of his sandwich and continue to the next harrowing image, at which point he simply repeated the process.

Breathing heavily, as he always had to in order to successfully oxygenate his vast physical mass, Morose wasn't in the best of moods. In fairness, he couldn't remember the last time he had been. Not really. But since the day of his arrest, and subsequent conviction for being what the papers had called The Psychotic Serial Slasher of Southampton and the South Coast, he'd been somewhat more belligerent than normal. This rather negative outlook on life had only been exacerbated by the certain knowledge that he wasn't, nor could he ever have been, The Psychotic Serial Slasher of Southampton and the South Coast. He'd known that then just as certainly as he knew it now, because he'd made the whole thing up, and he'd done so because, like every other Police Chief Inspector employed within the United Kingdom, he'd been working on a commission-based pay structure that just happened to favour murdered bodies over actual arrests. Subsequently, it had made good sense for him to link missing persons to every dead body the local hospital could provide him with at short notice, and after removing each body's head, hands and feet before presenting them to the missing persons' friends and family for formal identification, he'd been filling in his quarterly quota with almost gay abandon.

He'd probably have got away with it too, had he not thought it best to justify the huge numbers of murders they'd now been inundated with by asking one of his subordinates, a certain Detective Inspector Capstan, to organise a press conference to announce to the world that they had one of the most dangerous mass murderers on their hands since the Mouse Mass Murderer of Morden. Morose had taken the whole thing one step too far by publicising the press conference ahead of time through an anonymous email sent out to the nation's newspapers; but the email wasn't quite as anonymous as he'd expected it to be.

It was this that had made one particular investigative journalist more than a little suspicious; and after taking pictures of a pizza van picking up an assortment of body parts from the back of Solent Police Station late one evening, he'd sold the story to the tabloids, along with a copy of the not-so anonymous email Morose had sent out. He'd entitled his mailshot, "Morose, the Mass Murdering Chief Inspector of the Solent Police", and having recently completed a distance learning course in Criminal Psychology, the journalist had added a couple of paragraphs detailing exactly why Chief Inspector Morose was a mass murdering psychopath and therefore, *ipso facto*, was the elusive Psychotic Serial Slasher of Southampton and the South Coast for whom the police had apparently been searching.

The story was just too compelling not to be true, by British newspaper standards at any rate, and with the press convinced, it didn't take long to persuade the British Isle's sixty-three million other residents, along with the twelve eventually selected for jury duty and, of course, the judge presiding over the trial.

Between mouthfuls, and without looking up, the Warden eventually said, 'Take a seat, I'll be with you in a moment,' and turned over another page to stare at another picture of yet another severed head with matching pairs of hands and feet.

'I'd rather stand, if it's all the same to you,' replied Morose.

The Warden looked up from the file. 'You're not going to be one of those *difficult* prisoners, I hope?'

Morose had every intention of being just as difficult as possible, for the Prison Warden and everyone else he happened to set eyes on, and for the duration of the forty-two back-to-back life sentences he'd been so graciously given. However, his reluctance to sit had nothing to do with that; it was just that the wooden chair being offered was far too small for his immense size, and he doubted that it would be up to the job.

'I'd just prefer to stand, if it's all the same to you.'

Having acquainted himself with the man on paper, the Warden now took a moment to examine the giant figure looming before him.

'I must admit that I don't normally ask to see our newest arrivals,' he eventually said. 'But then again, it's not very often that we have the pleasure of entertaining an actual Police Chief Inspector! And certainly not one from the local community.'

With great effort, Morose didn't respond. Nor did he climb over the desk to give the Warden a warm, welcoming bear-hug that would squeeze the very life out of the man, as he'd certainly like to have done.

'I see you're a man of few words, which is probably best,' the Warden said, adding with a dry smile, 'I can't imagine you're going to be very popular around here.'

Again, Morose said nothing, but just continued to breathe in and out whilst doing his best to remain calm.

'In fact, it would probably be better for all concerned if you went into solitary confinement, at least until everyone got used to the idea of you being here.'

Still nothing from Morose.

'How long do you think it would take for your fellow inmates to accept you as one of their own, do you think? A couple of months? A year or two? Twenty or thirty, perhaps? It's difficult to know really, never having had someone of your former position in society here before. Tell you what, let's start with ten years' solitary confinement and see how everyone feels about you afterwards?'

Again, no comment came from Morose, and with a beaming grin, the Warden took a generous bite from his sandwich.

A few moments later he stopped and stared, very much like Morose had been doing, with his eyes ever-widening and his previously pallid countenance beginning to redden into what could probably best be described as puce.

He slapped his desk hard and stared up at Morose before using both hands to gesticulate at his throat. He was choking, probably on one of the many succulent bacon rashes that he'd been enjoying just moments before.

Morose observed the Warden, pondering what action he should take. If he were to offer his assistance by attempting to implement the Heimlich manoeuvre, but failed, as he was sure to do, as he'd only ever seen it done on TV, he'd probably be accused of yet another murder. The same went if he were to give him a hearty slap on the back. He could, of course, call for assistance, but somehow he had the feeling that, were the circumstances reversed, the Warden wouldn't do the same for him. So he decided to simply enjoy watching the man choke to death.

It only took another minute or two before he did so, and Morose found himself alone with the body of one who was the Warden of Portsmouth Prison no more. When absolutely certain the man was devoid of life, he turned to knock on the door, which opened pretty much straight away.

'That was quick,' said the Custodial Manager standing behind it, and was about to lead prisoner 3471 away to begin his forty-two back-to-back life sentences when he noticed the Warden, his head lying back on his chair, staring fixedly at the ceiling, with his tongue hanging half out of his mouth, and now looking more of a mauve colour than actual puce.

'My God!' exclaimed the man, 'What have you done?'

Morose rolled his eyes. Deep down he knew that whatever he'd done, or, once again, *hadn't* done, the result would have been the same, and the forty-two back-to-back life sentences would have simply been extended to forty-three.

'FRED!' shouted the man beside him, edging his way back from the hulking figure as he drew out his baton.

'FRED!' he called again, but this time with more urgency. He was definitely going to need back up with this one.

Moments later the Supervising Officer, who went by the name of Fred, came charging down the hall, baton at the ready.

'Hit the alarm - the Warden's been murdered!'

'Really?' asked Fred, as he caught his breath.

'Yes, of course, *really*! Do you think I'd make something like that up?'

'Well, no, but... Are you sure? I mean, it's never happened before.'

'Just because something's never happened before, doesn't mean it can't. See for yourself!' and he pointed at the body of the Warden, sitting very still behind his desk.

'And you think it was this man, do you?' asked Fred, staring up at Morose.

'Of course it was this man. Just look at the size of him!' They both gazed up in awe at inmate 3471.

Morose couldn't help himself; he grinned back down at them.

'Blimey, you're right,' said Fred. 'I'd better get some more back-up.'

'Well, hurry up. I can't hold him off all day!'

Morose sighed. He'd begun to wish he had at least tried to help the Warden. He may have even succeeded, and if so, he could have had his sentence reduced for...good behaviour, or something. But brought down to what? A forty-one year back-to-back life sentence?

He shrugged his shoulders again and mentally capitulated. If everyone in the world was forever going to automatically assume that he was a dangerous psychopathic mass murderer, even though he wasn't, he may as well start to act like one. Having made that paradigm shift in his thinking towards himself, and subsequently those around him, he stared back down at the now solitary Custodial Manager and said in a dark, ominous voice, 'You'd look good on a piece of bread, especially after I've sat on you, and you're dead.'

The man before him froze in all-consuming primordial fear.

Pleased with the result that actually speaking had on someone, Morose took one giant step towards him, pushed the guard to the ground and sat on him, a process which instantaneously crushed his ribcage, leading to massive internal haemorrhaging, deoxygenation, and, very shortly afterwards, death.

Delighted with what happened when he used someone as a beanbag, and feeling much better for having done what everyone had been accusing him of doing for the last nine months, Morose shifted his weight off of the Custodial Manager, found the key to undo his handcuffs, heaved himself back onto his feet and lumbered his way down the corridor to start becoming more familiar with his new surroundings.

Chapter Two
The new Number 10 Downing Street

09:24 BST

'ARE YOU ABSOLUTELY sure that this is the top floor?' asked Robert Bridlestock, the British Prime Minister, who'd arrived for work earlier than normal in order to see the view from his new office at the very top of what was Canary Wharf's HIGD Tower, but was now, officially, the brand new Number 10 Downing Street.

'I'm fairly sure it is, yes, Prime Minister,' replied Fredrick Overtoun, his long-standing Private Secretary.

With the side of his face pressed firmly up against the toughened glass window, Robert attempted to see if there was a floor above.

'I can see a bird standing on something up there,' he said. 'There must be another one on top of this.'

'I suspect that's the roof garden, Prime Minister. It's been converted into an open air restaurant, which is proving rather attractive to the pigeons.'

'Feathered little fuckers,' muttered Robert, removing his face and gazing out over Central London. 'Do you think I'd be able to see my golf course from here?'

'Isn't that in Kent, Prime Minister?'

'Yes, and?'

11

'I suspect it may just be a little too far away to see from Canary Wharf, even if we are in the penthouse suite of the top floor of one of the tallest buildings in the United Kingdom, Prime Minister.'

'Perhaps. But can you make a note to buy a telescope? I'd be much happier if I could keep an eye on it.'

'I'll add it to the list, Prime Minister.'

A pause in the conversation followed as Robert spent a few happy moments surveying what he considered to be his: the City of London, sprawled out before him, sparkling and shimmering in the early summer sunlight.

'Would now be a good time to go through the morning's newspapers, Prime Minister?'

'Is there *ever* a good time to go through the morning's newspapers, Fredrick?'

Choosing to ignore the remark and pulling out the first of many he had tucked under his arm, Fredrick said, 'There's an interesting story on the front page of the Financial Times, Prime Minister,' deliberately choosing that one as it was the only paper Robert would give so much as a courtesy glance to, were it up to him.

'Go on, then, let's have a look.' Robert made his way over to his gleaming new opaque glass desk with matching chrome and black leather executive arm chair, the very latest 27-inch iMac monitor that sat with perfect engineered precision on the right-hand side of the glass top, and a sleek black desk phone on the left.

Unfolding the newspaper, Fredrick laid it out so

that they could both clearly see the headline, which was so big it would have been difficult to miss; but just to make sure Robert couldn't, Fredrick read it out.

'It says, "WHEN THE BREX'SHIT HITS THE FAN," Prime Minister.'

'Yes, I can see that, thank you, Fredrick.'

'It goes on to say that the pound still hasn't recovered from the 31 year low it sank to when the Referendum results were announced on Friday, and that the FTSE 100 index remains in steady decline, Prime Minister.'

'Well, sod the FT. They're not always right. What does The Sun say?'

Pulling that one out, Fredrick said, 'They're not leading with a story about you, Prime Minister. They're still talking about the football match on Saturday.'

Robert looked none the wiser.

'England's defeat against the Chelsea Pensioners, Prime Minister. Didn't you hear about it?' asked Fredrick, with renewed incredulity for his boss's lack of interest in absolutely everything, except golf and his personal net worth.

'I didn't even know the Chelsea Pensioners had a football team.'

'It was a charity match, but even so, there was a general expectation that England should win it, given the fact that the average age of their opponents was ninety-four. It was also fairly evident that England was having a go at it, and it wasn't as if they didn't have their chances,' continued Fredrick, who happened to enjoy watching the odd match from the comfort of his living room sofa, 'but the Chelsea Pensioners' defence was just too strong, and England were simply unable to convert anything into a goal.'

'Well, at least there's nothing disparaging in there about me!'

'Unfortunately there is, Prime Minister. You're on page three.'

'What on earth am I doing on page three?'

'Nothing, Prime Minister. You're just smiling at the camera, but the headline reads, "OUR BIGGEST TIT, EVER!"'

Robert visibly sagged. He wasn't used to being berated by The Sun. No matter how deep the cesspit was that he'd previously managed to lead his country into, they'd historically always backed him up.

'But you'll be pleased to hear that all the other papers *have* decided to feature you on the front page,' continued Fredrick, as he pulled each one out from under his arm and proceeded to pile them up on the PM's desk, reading out their various headlines as he did so.

'The Observer went with, "Time to go", The Times says, "Rob the Knob", The Telegraph's gone with, "Bob another Job", The Daily Star's taken a more consultatory route with, "Sponge Bob Square Pants for Prime Minister". The Independent says, "I, Knob'ert", which I can only assume is a satirical jibe at your book; and The Daily Mail's decided to base their headline on what I believe is a traditional football chant,' and he read out, '"Robert is a Knobert, Robert is a Knobert, tra-la la la, tra-la la la,"' in a flat, monotonous tone. 'Oh, and I also picked up a copy of The Independent Socialist On Monday, simply because they're offering

£50 to anyone who's willing to assassinate you.'

Robert gave Fredrick a curious look of surprised alarm.

'Don't worry, Prime Minister, it's unlikely anyone would, not for such a small amount at any rate, but it may be worth taking on some additional security, just until things settle down a little.'

Robert eased himself down onto his chair and began picking through the papers as though they were a pile of freshly-donated charity shop clothes. He was more than used to the odd derogatory remark levelled at him by the Nation's press, but this was on a whole new level.

'But I— I don't understand, Fredrick. Why has everyone suddenly turned against me?'

'I suspect,' said Fredrick, electing to choose his words carefully, 'it's the unfortunate culmination of things all sort of happening at once, Prime Minister. The Times featuring you at the top of their UK Rich List last Thursday didn't exactly go down well. Then Friday we had the European Referendum results, so we'll now have to leave the EU, which, apart from the entire population of Birmingham, most seem to think is a backwards step that will lead us straight into another recession. The Party itself remains mystified as to why you called it in the first place, let alone your decision to then lead the "Leave" campaign which such unusual vigour. And over the weekend, of course, we moved out of Number 10 Downing Street, having sold it to an American banker, and we're now based in what used to be Canary Wharf's HIGD Tower, one of the largest and most expensive buildings in the United

Kingdom, of which you have the Penthouse Suite, Prime Minister.'

'Well, at least they can't blame me for the football,' retorted Robert.

'Unfortunately, they do seem to be laying that at your feet as well, Prime Minister.'

'How on earth can that be my fault?'

'The Sun seems to think that it's the result of you persuading the National Lottery to only offer grants to sports that use balls, and then only spherical shaped ones that have a maximum diameter of 1.68 inches, which just happens to be the exact same size as those used for playing golf. And they've gone on to propose that that's why today's youth seem more interested in playing that game than any other, leaving a formerly prosperous England Football Squad somewhat short on players, equipment, sponsors and half-decent managers. They've summarised their current position by saying that England's defeat by Lithuania in the first round of the European Championship, and now of course their having lost to The Chelsea Pensioners, is, indeed, *your fault*, Prime Minister.'

Robert pushed himself away from his desk, stood up, and began to pace up and down the generously-spaced office suite, with his hands clasped firmly behind his back.

'It may be better to stay away from the windows, Prime Minister, just in case someone else has bought a copy of The Independent Socialist On Monday.'

'Oh, c'mon, Fredrick, now you're just being silly.'

'And before we've had approval from the Cabinet to install bullet-proof glass,' continued Fredrick, with the solemn benevolence of a man waiting for another man to be shot in the head, so that he could read out his pre-prepared eulogy.

At that moment something hit the window, probably a fly, and they both ducked instinctively.

'Jesus Christ, I can't work like this. You'd better get some blinds fitted, at least until the windows can be upgraded.'

'Yes, Prime Minister. I'll make a note to get some, along with the telescope.'

Deciding to heed his Private Secretary's advice for once, and not to continually pace up and down beside the huge window, like an over-sized mechanical pigeon at the end of a fairground shooting alley, Robert returned to his desk.

'Dare I ask what the Cabinet thinks about all this?'

'About installing bullet-proof glass, Prime Minister?'

'Of course not! About my plunging popularity?'

'I'm not sure, Prime Minister, but in these situations they normally advise on a course of immediate resignation.'

'Well, sod that for a game of soldiers. I'll leave when I want to, and I'm buggered if I'm going to be pushed out just because we lost the odd game of football.'

'Perhaps then I should arrange for you to meet with them, Prime Minister?'

'Who? The England Football team?'

'No, Prime Minister. The Cabinet.'

'Is that really necessary? Can't you just email them a questionnaire, or something?'

'They'd probably appreciate it if you did take the time to meet with them this time, Prime Minister. It would be unfortunate if they were to decide to push for a Parliamentary vote of no confidence and have you forced out, without at least giving you the chance to persuade them otherwise.'

'Oh, very well. You'd better arrange it. But not for today! I feel like I need cheering up, and I suspect a meeting with that lot would be more likely to send me into a bout of clinical depression.'

As the PM's brand new phone began to burble away on his desk, Fredrick said, 'Surely not, Prime Minister,' and with a hidden smile, reached down to pick up the receiver. 'Prime Minister's office?'

After a moment's pause he covered the mouthpiece with one hand and whispered, 'Your niece is down in the lobby, asking if she can come up.'

'Claire? Just what the doctor ordered! She'll only want to borrow more money, but at least she's *fun*, which is more than I can say for anyone around here. Yes, send her up!'

'Right away, Prime Minister.'

'And then you'd better unpack my drinks cabinet. God knows I could do with one!'

Chapter Three
Charity begins six hundred feet up

09:37 BST

'CLAIRE BRIDLESTOCK to see you, Prime Minister,' said Fredrick, as he stood aside to let Robert's niece breeze in, looking very much like a Channel 5 Late Night Weathergirl.

'Thanks, Freddie,' she said, as she brushed past, turning to add, 'You're looking very well. Have you done something with your hair?'

'Oh… um… er,' replied Fredrick, as he went a rather obvious shade of red. He wasn't used to anyone paying him the slightest bit of attention, let alone the Prime Minister's twenty-three year old niece, who wouldn't have looked out of place on the cover of Cosmo.

'Hello, Claire,' called Robert, staring over at her with his tongue already half out of his mouth.

Like most men, he always found himself slipping into a hypnotic state of deep sexual arousal whenever she walked into the same room, which was something that had worried him for some time, not because she was young enough to be his daughter, but because she stood a very good chance of actually being so.

Back in the day, he'd found himself seeing quite a lot more of his brother's soon-to-be wife than he'd

19

initially expected to, and they'd started to happily bonk each other only minutes after being introduced during the engagement party. And furthermore, at the time, his preferred method of contraception was what his university college termed "extraculation", which was great in theory, but rarely worked in practice, especially after a bottle or two of vino.

'Hello, Uncle Bob,' she said, with a beguiling smile, which worried him even more, seeing that it was looking increasingly like his own each time he saw her.

She dumped her obligatory five shopping bags down on top of his desk and asked, 'How's running the country treating you?' before pushing her breasts up against him and giving his cheek an enchanting kiss.

'Oh, you know. It has its moments.'

'Well, you don't seem to be very popular at the moment.'

'What makes you say that?'

'Oh, I don't know, but probably the ninety thousand or so people currently marching through London burning effigies of you.'

'Is that true, Fredrick?' he asked, staring at his Private Secretary, who hovered beside the office door as he was paid to.

'I'm sorry, Prime Minister. I must have forgotten to mention it.'

'And was it really necessary to sell Number 10?' she asked, stepping over to the wall-to-wall window. 'I mean, it was a national icon, and it's taken me bloody ages to get all the way up here.'

'Yes, well, unfortunately we were made an offer we couldn't refuse.'

'Then you should have tried a little harder, don't you think?' she said, gazing out over Canary Wharf and the City of London beyond. 'Anyway, what floor are we on?'

'The top one,' answered Robert, with a proud smile.

'Are you sure?' she asked, looking up to see if there was a floor above, but being careful not to smudge her makeup on the glass. 'There's a pigeon standing on something up there.'

'That's the rooftop restaurant.'

Clearing his throat, Fredrick said, 'If you don't mind me saying so, Miss Bridlestock, but it may be wise to stay away from the windows.'

She turned to look questioningly at him.

'It's just that the, er, The Independent Socialist On Monday has offered £50 for anyone willing to, um, assassinate...' and he used his eyes to indicate to whom he was referring.

'Yes, thank you, Fredrick,' said Robert, 'but you really don't need to go around telling everyone.'

Ignoring the threat on her uncle's life, but deciding to heed the council of his Private Secretary, Claire made her way over to the black leather and chrome square-edged sofas that surrounded a large rectangular opaque glass coffee table in the centre of the vast office suite.

Sitting down, she crossed her legs, put both arms over the back of the sofa, looked up at Robert and asked, 'And why on earth did you think it was a great idea to leave the EU, Uncle? You do know that just about everything half-decent comes from there, don't you?'

'That's not entirely true, now, is it, Claire?'

'Yes, it bloody is! Everything I eat, drink and wear is either from Italy or France. All the best cars are German, my moped is Italian, the furniture in my flat is Swedish, most of my friends are from Europe and Daddy's yacht is French. In fact, I can't think of a single thing that actually does come from the UK that's worth talking about.'

'Golf does,' said Robert, feeling both defensive and patriotic at the same time.

'It originated from Scotland, Uncle. I'm not sure that counts.'

She was right, of course, but he didn't think she'd have known that.

'What about football?' he asked. He really had no idea. 'And cricket,' he added, with more certainty. 'Oh, and there's rugby, of course.'

He was on a roll, and concluded his argument by adding, 'Not to mention the Dyson vacuum cleaner!'

Claire frowned at him.

'We also invented sandwiches,' he continued, 'and I'm fairly sure we came up with the idea of the biscuit!'

'That's as may be,' she said, 'but it will certainly be quite a diplomatic challenge to enter the fray of international commerce as a brand new non-member of the European Union with the only items available for trade being a trendy-looking vacuum cleaner and a packet of Hobnobs. I'm no politician, but even I can understand the all too obvious benefits of being inside the EU as opposed to being out of it, which was why we signed up for it in the first place, surely?'

Robert wasn't used to being berated quite so

articulately by his very own niece, a girl who it didn't seem all that long ago was running around his swimming pool with nothing on but a John Lewis nappy.

Keen to change the subject, he asked, 'Would you like a drink, my dear?' and looked over at Fredrick, still standing beside the door but now with a distinct air of smugness about him.

'I suppose it depends on what you have,' she said. 'If it's a toss-up between Newcastle Brown Ale and a pint of Portsmouth Pride, I think I'd rather up sticks and move to Paris.'

'Fredrick, did you have a chance to unpack the drinks cabinet?'

'Not quite, Prime Minister, but I think I can offer Miss Bridlestock a glass of Château d'Yquem.'

'Oh, go on then,' she said, 'but do please note that with a name like Château d'Yquem it's probably French, and so, by definition, comes from France, and now that we're leaving the EU, voluntarily I may add, it will cost at least twice as much next year, along with everything else!'

'If you could fetch us two glasses, thank you, Fredrick.'

'Yes, Prime Minister.' Fredrick slunk out of the office to try and find the crates that they'd packed all the wine into on Friday afternoon.

'So, Claire,' said Robert with his usual conversational charm, 'how's your degree going?'

'I finished it last year,' she said, opening her Gucci handbag to begin an in-depth search for her iPhone.

'I thought you'd only just started?'

With the phone found she snapped the bag shut and glared at him.

'I'd been there for four bloody years!'

'Well, yes, I suppose you had. I must admit that I have slipped behind with the family news a little since moving into office.'

'No kidding!' she said, and tapped her iPhone's social media icon, adding, 'Did you know that out of all my two thousand, four hundred and fifty-two Facebook friends, only three of them were actually born in England?'

'I didn't know that, no. So, anyway, what did you get?'

'What "what" did I get?'

'Your degree? What did you end up with?'

'Oh, that. I got a first.'

'That's outstanding. Well done!' exclaimed Robert, hoping to lift her mood a little.

Claire shrugged. 'It was in Social Media, so getting a first was mandatory. We all got one.'

'I see. And what have you been doing since then?'

'I set up my own PR firm,' she answered, scrolling through her Facebook newsfeed.

'Really?' asked Robert, unable to hide his surprise.

'Yes, really!' she said, glaring up at him. 'Don't look at me like that!'

'I wasn't looking at you like anything.'

'Yes, you were. You were looking at me as if it was probably against the law for a young girl, fresh out of university, to start her own business, and if it wasn't, then it should be, and that you were about to pop downstairs to pass a bill to make sure that it was.'

She put away her iPhone and rummaged around for her compact.

'So,' asked Robert, 'how's business? Do you have many clients?'

'A few,' she said, giving her face a quick once-over.

'Have I heard of any of them?'

'Probably not. My main one is a small start-up charity firm.'

'Oh, really? What's it called?'

'Blind Dogs for the Guides.'

'Blind Dogs for the Guides?' repeated Robert, unsure if he'd heard it correctly.

'Yes, that's right.'

'I see. And what do they do?'

'They provide blind dogs for the Girl Guides, obviously!'

'And there's a demand for that, is there?'

'We're looking at it as being an untapped market.'

'Wouldn't it have been better if they gave *normal* dogs to the Guides, instead of blind ones?'

'Perhaps, but it wouldn't have been much of a charity then, would it? Their idea was to find blind dogs who were in need of a good home, and then donate them to suitable groups of Girl Guides who'd be able to provide them with one.'

'That makes sense, I suppose. And how's it all going?'

'To be honest, not great. The launch party went really well, but after everyone had sobered up and realised that they weren't Guide Dogs for the Blind, as they'd first thought, we had a number of people asking for their money back. And then there was the unfortunate incident when their first dog decided to help a group of Girl Guides to cross the M4, and it proved a little tricky to find anyone willing to run a positive article about them afterwards, which is why I thought I'd pop in to see you.'

'I see. Would you like me to put in a good word for them?'

'Not really. They're pretty much dead in the water. So anyway, I've decided that running a business really isn't my thing after all, so I was wondering if you had something I could do around here.'

'A job, you mean?'

'Yes, one of those.'

'I must admit that I thought you'd simply come up to borrow some money.'

'I did, but I'd like a job as well, if it's not too much trouble.'

'And what sort of thing did you have in mind?'

'Well, judging by how the entire country seems to hate you, I thought you could do with a bit of marketing and public relations support. Something to lift your image a little.'

Robert looked up to see Fredrick come in carrying two glasses and a bottle of what he assumed was the Château d'Yquem.

'Ah, there you are Fredrick. Do you think my current situation would benefit from a bit of marketing and PR?'

Placing the already opened £5,000 bottle of wine down carefully onto the glass coffee table, Fredrick said, 'I can't imagine it could do you any harm, Prime Minister.'

'Excellent! Then I'd like to propose a toast.' Robert filled the glass nearest to Claire's to the brim before pouring one for himself. He then stood up and raised his own to announce, 'To my niece, Claire Bridlestock, my new Marketing and PR Consultant.'

Claire also stood, but before joining in with the toast, asked, 'How much are you offering?'

'Oh, er— How much do you want?'

'I was thinking along the lines of £50,000.'

'That much?' responded Robert. 'How about we start you off on £12,000, and see how you get on.'

'Are you joking? I got paid more than that as a babysitter! How about £45,000?'

'£15,000?'

'£40,000?'

'£20,000?'

'£35,000?'

'£25,000?'

'£30,000?'

'Done!' declared Robert, feeling exceptionally pleased with himself. 'When can you start?'

'I'd need to go shopping first, of course. Sometime next month?'

'How about tomorrow, at nine.'

'What, in the morning?'

'Perhaps that is a little early,' agreed Robert. 'Shall we say eleven?'

'That will do,' said Claire. She'd never been much of one for getting up before lunchtime, but needs must when the Devil drives, and her father had issued her with a final warning the previous day that if she didn't come up with some way to make a sensible living, and preferably one that didn't involve finding short-sighted dogs willing and able to lead Girl Guides to their certain deaths, then he'd be cutting her allowance in half before the week was out.

Chapter Four
All the King's Horses

09:46 BST

NEWS OF PORTSMOUTH Prison's Warden's early demise at the hands of Morose, the former Chief Inspector of the Solent Police, had spread to all those serving time at Her Majesty's pleasure in prisons the length and breadth of the British Isles, thanks solely to the prohibited use of Social Media.

Over recent years, the dependence on Facebook, Twitter, and the like, within people's normal lives outside the prison walls was an addiction the vast majority of new inmates were simply unable to give up, and subsequently the illicit trade in smartphones was now on an equal footing with cigarettes, alcohol and PlayStation 3 bundled with Tour of Duty. In other words, everyone had one, and the British prison service had long since turned a blind eye.

Subsequently, by the time Morose had discovered a coffee machine at the end of the strangely empty corridor he'd been strolling down, realised he didn't have any money to buy one, gone back to where the Custodial Manager lay flattened out beside the Warden's still open office door, rummaged through his pockets to find a one pound coin, ambled back to the coffee machine, inserted the coin, pressed the relevant

29

button and extracted what was described as an Authentically Flavoured Mexican Golden Roasted Cappuccino, Morose heard a cheer go up closely followed by what could best be described as a bit of a ruckus. Having nothing better to do, he lumbered his way towards it, with a nonchalant hand shoved into a pocket and the other holding the coffee.

He soon discovered that the noise, which had grown considerably louder as he'd progressed towards it, came from what must be the communal area. As he strolled in he looked up and around to see that it was flanked on either side by three rows of steel-grated gantries, each one lined with prisoners, all shouting over the space between them in a way remarkably similar to a Parliamentary debate.

It wasn't long before one of them caught his eye, and the malnourished-looking man began tugging on the jacket of the prisoner beside him whilst pointing at Morose, exclaiming, 'It's him! Look! Down there! It's him! Look! There! It's him! Down there! Look! It's him! Right there! Look! It's him! Down there! It's him! Look! There! It's him! Down there! Look! It's him! There! Right there! It's him! There! Right there! Look!' but eventually gave up, having come to the conclusion that no matter how hard he pulled on the coat of the prisoner next to him, or how many times he repeated, "It's him! Look! Down there!" he was never going to achieve his ultimate goal of making at least one other person aware of Morose's presence by doing so. So instead he cupped his hands together and bellowed, 'CHIEF INSPECTOR MOROSE IS DOWN THERE, YOU BUNCH OF FUCKING RETARDS!'

As everyone turned to stare at just who it was, exactly, who'd called them all a bunch of fucking retards, the scrawny-looking man pointed straight at Morose and added, 'He's down there!' in order to justify his almost unprecedented outburst.

Since Portsmouth's prison population had received the tweet that the Warden had been murdered at the hands of Morose just twenty minutes earlier, anarchy had reigned supreme and the remaining prison officers had been beaten up and left for dead inside one of the larger prison cells.

The prison had then divided.

The inmates now standing on the left-hand side gantries were all those who'd been put in there as the direct result of one of Morose's many schemes to increase his quarterly bonus. As a collective mass they all felt rather sorry for the Warden. They may not have liked him much, but being strangled to death wasn't something they'd wish on anyone; and they were now desperate to see Morose pay the ultimate price for both the Warden's demise and their own incarceration, and were looking forward to sticking his head on a spike outside the prison gates, preferably just besides the intercom button used by the visitors to gain access.

However, those who'd never heard of Morose, not before his arrest and public trial at any rate, but knew all too well of their spiteful, belittling Warden, Mr Oliver Obtuse, thought it was the best news they'd ever heard in their entire lives, and were all rather keen to meet this Morose character and shake him by the hand.

An eerie silence fell over the hundreds of prisoners, as they leaned out over the three high metal gantries, all looking down at the communal area where stood the solitary figure of an immensely fat middle-aged man with one hand in his pocket and the other holding what looked to be a nice hot cup of coffee.

Feeling a little embarrassed by all the sudden attention, Morose gave them all a sheepish smile, lifted his drink and said, 'Cheers!' by way of formal introduction.

A huge bellow of approval erupted from the right-hand side of the on-lookers whilst a series of disgruntled boos came thundering down from the left. As they all began to bang their obligatory prison-issue metal mugs on the railings, Morose couldn't help but observe that the whole ensemble now sounded very much like a steel band doing a modern variation of the ever-popular Queen anthem, "We Will Rock You," which was one of his personal favourites.

As he began to feel increasingly more at home, a short, well-groomed, and equally well-fed gentleman with slicked back grey hair and an out of place suntan, wearing a precision-pressed prison uniform, a blue tie and a highly polished pair of black leather shoes, began to gracefully descend one of the many flights of gantry steps towards the communal area where Morose stood, enjoying his coffee.

Following close behind were two giant men who were keeping a watchful eye on the fat, well-dressed little chap in front of them, and everyone else.

When he reached the ground floor, he raised both his hands to placate the hordes of overhanging prisoners, who soon fell back into silence.

'Chief Inspector Morose,' he called out. 'What an honour it is to have you here among us.'

'If it isn't Harry Humpty,' said Morose, through a scornful grin. 'I was wondering which enormous pile of crap you'd been hidden under, and I see it's this one.'

Harry Humpty, known throughout the Criminal Underworld as Humpty the Dumpty, not because he'd ever had a great fall or anything, but because of his name, and the fact that he looked remarkably like a highly-evolved free-range egg, was the Head of the Centre for Organised Crime and Kidnapping, otherwise known as COCK for short. This was an acronym chosen quite deliberately to cause maximum embarrassment whenever they were being discussed by either the nation's police force or by the many solicitors, judges and lawyers of the land who relied on their multitude of subversive criminal activities to keep them in full-time employment. And as if to make the point, Humpty said, 'Have you heard what my COCK's been up to lately?'

The assembled criminal masses all roared with laughter as Morose returned a wry smile. He neither knew, nor cared, what the Centre for Organised Crime and Kidnapping had been up to recently, and hadn't done since their formation back in the early 1950s.

'Hasn't anyone told you?' said Morose. 'I'm now, officially, the Psychotic Serial Slasher of Southampton and the South Coast, and I just strangled the Warden with my bare hands. So as hard as it is to believe, I reckon I'm now an even bigger cock than you are!'

Certain members of the audience couldn't help themselves and a handful of titters and guffaws trickled down from the gantries above, but they were all quickly supressed, voluntarily or otherwise.

'Yes, and we'd certainly like to thank you for your assistance with the dispatching of the Warden, but we've since dealt with all the guards, and I can now safely say that Portsmouth Prison is in the hands of us, the prisoners; and to be frank, you're not included.'

Morose took a moment to take a sip from his coffee before speaking again.

'May I ask what your intentions are now?'

'Well, after throwing you from the highest gantry,' answered Humpty, gazing up at his doting audience, 'the first thing we're going to do is order pizza. Isn't that right, lads?'

A huge cheer went up from around the prison, as the inmates all began salivating and wondering when they could expect delivery.

'And what then?' asked Morose, after the noise had died down.

'Er,' replied Humpty, who hadn't really thought beyond lunchtime.

Looking up to the assembled masses, Morose began to address them.

'Many of you know the man I used to be,' he called up, and then waited for more than the odd defamatory remark to come bouncing back down again, before continuing, 'but I suspect that only a few of you know who I've since become.'

Silence followed, but as they'd all been following the case on Twitter, they had a pretty good idea.

'And if further evidence is needed, it can be found sitting in the Warden's chair where, allegedly, I murdered him with my bare hands.'

Some of the disgruntlement now changed to murmurs of approval, and to encourage this, Morose added, 'Fortunately he didn't seem to mind too much.'

Ripples of laughter followed.

'After dealing with the Warden, I also disposed of one of the guards. Now, I would ask him to vouch for me, but I'm told he's a little short of breath, and that he will be for quite some time.'

More titters of amusement could be heard.

'I know that many of you are here because of me, but that's just tough shit! My former job was commission-based, so I had no choice.'

As a large number of those he was addressing had worked in Sales at some point during their previous lives, they could at least understand his position, even if they couldn't agree with it.

'If you accept me as one of your own,' continued Morose, 'I promise, first and foremost, to negotiate a highly favourable deal for you. I know the police, and I understand their ways, so I can guarantee that you can get whatever it is that you want, be it a pizza, a Happy Meal, a Big Mac with a strawberry shake and fries, or even a KFC Chicken Bucket! But I say, why stop there? We have a unique opportunity here, and one that we can use to make the system pay for putting us all inside, and I mean *all* of us! My proposal is this. Instead of treating this place as a prison to enslave us, we start thinking of it as a castle from which we can fight. Look at it! It's an impregnable fortress, and from this vantage point we can defend our borders whilst exacting our revenge on the society that put us here. From the safety of these walls we can steal the cars, rob the banks, hold up the trains, import the drugs, manage the brothels, and kidnap the rich; and all the while giving back to us, the poor of heart, at least. So, what I propose is this. First we ask for a menu, and then we get busy. How about it?'

A giant roar went up from the gantries which soon turned into the chant of, "Mor-ose! Mor-ose! Mor-ose! Mor-ose!"

As his name rang out along the many corridors and into every cell, the entire prison population began piling down the gantry steps to welcome their new inmate into the fold.

Reaching the ground floor, half of them started to take it in turns to introduce themselves to Morose, whilst the others, with the help of the two bodyguards, lifted Mr Humpty up above their heads and carried him all the way to the very highest gantry.

Soon the cry of, 'MIND YOUR HEADS!' echoed down, as Humpty the Dumpty had the great fall he'd been destined to have since birth, and splatted out in the middle of the ground floor, where neither King's Horse, nor King's Men, had a chance in hell of putting him back together again, even if one of them did happen to have opposing thumbs and a limitless supply of surgical tape.

Chapter Five
Pets and presents

13:26 BST

'*Capstan, is that you?*'

With a sigh heavy enough to sink a plastic duck, Capstan said, 'C'mon Dewbush, we'd better see what he wants,' and pivoted around to head back towards the office door that they'd only just attempted to slip past without being noticed.

'Right you are, Sir,' replied Dewbush, who did a quick one hundred and eighty degree turn to follow on after.

'Are, there you are! Do, please, come in.'

Occupying the space behind what used to be Morose's desk just nine months earlier sat the Solent Police's relatively new man in charge, Chief Inspector Chupples.

This wasn't something Capstan was particularly happy about. He hadn't been since arriving back from his brief incarceration inside a German military prison cell, where he'd been forcibly hung upside down besides his virtually undead, half-brained, vampire-like subordinate, Sergeant Dewbush, who'd spent his time challenging his boss's intellect through the subtle machinations of I-Spy. It was for that reason, and the attempted arrest of a certain Jill Meadowbank

37

afterwards, that he'd been too late getting his own job application in for the position in question.

But if he was honest with himself, which he never was, of course, but if he had been, then, deep down, Capstan knew that he wasn't the right man for the job anyway. He could hardly be bothered to do his current one, let alone take on the many challenges and responsibilities that would have inevitably come with the Police Chief Inspector's position. This had been made all the more apparent by the fastidious passion that the man chosen in his absence had injected into the role.

Unlike Morose, Chupples was an honest, upright, hard-working and dedicated policeman whose love for the job had brought a level of police efficiency rarely seen in any British constabulary, let alone the Solent's. Capstan, of course, would never have done that. He wouldn't have even shown the ambitious drive that had led Morose down the blood-splattered slope to his present situation either. He'd probably have just sat there thinking up new methods of advanced police delegation.

But if life working as a Detective Inspector for the Solent Constabulary had been a little dull under the former Chief Inspector, Les Miserable himself, Chupples' ascendancy to the throne had made those days seem like being trapped inside a game of Grand Theft Auto.

'And how are you both?' asked Chupples.

'Very well, thank you, Sir,' answered Capstan.

'I'm very well too, thank you for asking,' chipped in Dewbush, never keen to be left out.

'What are you working on at the moment?'

'We're still on that dog case, Sir,' replied Capstan.

'The missing one?'

'Yes, that one, Sir.'

'I see,' said Chupples, placing his elbows on his desk and entwining his fingers together. 'Any clues?'

'Not as such, Sir, no. But Dewbush thought he may have heard it when we were walking past Burnside Allotments yesterday, Sir.'

'Ah! Okay, hold on a sec.' He used his mouse to open the folder on his computer's desktop labelled "Missing Pets".

'What's the dog's name?'

'Er, it's Pencil Case, Sir.'

'Ah yes, here it is. And when did you say you heard it?'

'It was yesterday afternoon, Sir. At around ten past three.'

'And did you see it, or just hear it?'

'We only heard it, Sir. At least we thought we did, but in fairness it could have been another dog, Sir, and possibly one of the others that has recently gone missing.'

'It would seem that we've had a fair few of them at the moment,' acknowledged Chupples. 'Two this week already, and four last month! It's all well over our expected quota.' With a sagacious frown, he leaned back in the black executives' chair that would have creaked and groaned under the immense strain to which Morose used to subject it, but with Chupples it just squeaked a bit. 'Have you had a chance to speak to the owner?'

'We've had a chat to the man, yes, Sir.'

'And was he able to throw any light on the subject?'

'Not really,' replied Capstan, as he stared out of the small office window.

Detective Inspector Capstan was unconditionally, categorically, incomprehensibly and completely bored by this conversation, and every other one he'd had with their new Chief Inspector, ever since Morose had been carted away.

Once Chupples had taken over, what had historically always been a low-crime area had now become one in which no criminal activity ever seemed to take place, and the entire Solent constabulary had little else to do but walk around all day looking for lost dogs and picking up litter. Life had become so sedentary that a number had already left to seek more action-packed careers as traffic wardens. At least Capstan still had the odd fight outside a night club to deal with, but even they were on the decline since Chupples had launched a new poster campaign that stated, "If you punch someone outside a nightclub, without asking their permission first, you'll get an £80 penalty," which was proving to be remarkably effective.

'Did he at least elaborate on the circumstances?' asked Chupples.

'He did Sir, yes. He said that he'd taken his dog for a walk after lunch, but when it ran off, chasing a squirrel, or something, he was too embarrassed to go around shouting, "Pencil Case, Pencil Case, has anyone seen my Pencil Case," so he just came straight home and dialled 999, Sir.'

'I see.'

As Chupples thought that one over, Capstan added, 'So the recent spate of missing dogs could be down to the current trend of naming pets after inanimate household objects, Sir.'

'Right,' said Chupples, gazing up at the ceiling in deep, meditative contemplation.

'And that would also explain,' continued Capstan, 'why we've had all those calls about so-called "deranged nut-jobs" wondering around town asking if anyone's seen their Toaster, Toothbrush or Clothes Peg, Sir.'

'And the Washing Machine one as well, Sir,' chipped in Dewbush, who'd begun to leaf through the relevant section of his notebook.

Chupples' desk phone started to ring, and with his exalted level of concentration now broken, the relatively new Chief Inspector leaned forward in his chair, reached over his immaculately clean, tidy desk, and picked up the receiver.

'Chupples here!' he said, leaning back again. But as he listened he gradually eased himself forward until both elbows were back on the desk.

'The Warden?' he asked, followed by an incredulous, 'Are you sure? I've never heard that happen before.'

There was another lengthy pause that ended with him asking, 'And it was definitely Morose? I see. Right, I'll send some men down straight away.'

With the receiver back in its cradle he stared at Capstan, who was unusually curious to find out what the call had been about.

'It would appear that our Morose has been up to no good again,' said Chupples.

'I thought he was in prison, Sir?'

'Yes, he is. He started his sentence at nine this morning, but by half past he'd already managed to murder the Prison Warden with his bare hands and then, somehow, did something similar to the Custodial Manager!'

'Perhaps he didn't mean to, Sir,' said Sergeant Dewbush, rallying to Morose's defence. 'Perhaps he did it by accident?' He'd always liked his former Chief Inspector, but probably only because he'd never been at the sharp end of his chronic misery.

'Well, it's possible, I suppose,' mused Chupples, 'but it's difficult to imagine how anyone could kill two people in quick succession without actually meaning to. Anyway, it gets worse, I'm afraid. A riot's now broken out and the prisoners have taken all remaining Prison Guards hostage. You two had better get over there. Find out what they want, try to calm the situation down, and whatever you do, don't let the press anywhere near the place! Do you understand?'

'Yes, Sir,' said Capstan.

'What about Pencil Case,' asked Dewbush, 'and all the other missing dogs, Sir?'

'You'll have to leave them for now, Sergeant, but I'm sure they'll still be here when you get back.'

'But what if they're not, Sir? They could easily wander up to the M27, and if they did that, then we'd *never* find them, Sir.'

'Perhaps, Sergeant, but I don't think it's likely, and even if they did, I can't imagine they'd do any harm.'

'They would if they all tried to cross it at once, during rush-hour, Sir.'

Sensing a rare opportunity to get rid of his Sergeant for the rest of the day, Capstan proposed a solution.

'Perhaps Dewbush could stay here and continue with the missing dog case, Sir, whilst I head off to attend the riot?'

'No, I want you both down at the prison. That must take priority for now, I'm afraid.'

'I know, Sir!' exclaimed Dewbush, who'd just been struck by what he knew with absolute certainty to be a really good idea. 'Perhaps we could continue searching for the dogs when we're at the Prison, Sir? We haven't had a chance to look down there yet, and that could be where they've been hiding, Sir.'

'An excellent idea, Sergeant. Well done! You see, Capstan, this is what we need. Policemen who can think on their feet!'

Capstan knew that the only reason Dewbush was able to think on his feet was because he was standing on them. However, not being one to contradict his superior, not without a fair amount of provocation at any rate, he said, 'Yes, Sir,' and glanced at his Sergeant. 'In fact, Sir,' he added, 'I've suspected for some time that our Sergeant Dewbush here is a gifted genius of the very highest order, Sir.'

'Right, good. Well, off you pop then. And do let me know how you get on at the prison.'

'And we'll call in if we have any news on those dogs, Sir,' said Dewbush, as they took a step backwards, turned and marched out of the office.

With the Chief Inspector's door firmly closed,

Dewbush asked, 'Do you really think I'm a genius of the highest order, Sir?'

'No, Dewbush. You're a dysfunctional moronic fuck-wit, as you well know. Now c'mon. Let's head over to the prison and see what's going on down there.'

As Dewbush tried to figure out what his boss really thought about him, a gifted genius or a dysfunctional moronic fuck-wit, as was Capstan's normal and all-too-rather-often expressed opinion, they made their way down the stairs to the Solent Police Station's lobby and out into the carpark at the front of the building.

As they approached their unmarked midnight blue BMW, Dewbush asked, 'Would you mind if we stopped by Waitrose on the way, Sir?'

'But we've only just had lunch!'

'I know, Sir, but I thought we could pick up some grapes.'

'Grapes?'

'Yes, Sir. For Morose, Sir. I thought that as we haven't seen him in such a long time, it would be nice if we could give him a little something, Sir.'

'He's not in hospital with a broken leg; you do know that, don't you, Sergeant?'

'Yes, Sir, but I still think he'd appreciate it if we did.'

'I suspect the only gift Morose would appreciate would be a cake with an iron file stuck in it.'

'Either some grapes or the cake, Sir, but I do think we should get him something.'

'Fair enough. There's a Waitrose on the way; and maybe we could pick up a dog whistle and a net whilst we're there.'

Chapter Six
Portsmouth Prison

13:58 BST

'IT LOOKS QUIET enough, Sir,' observed Dewbush, clutching a small green and white Waitrose paper bag that contained the grapes they'd bought on the way.

They were surveying the historic Portsmouth Prison from behind the ten foot high security fence that surrounded its ancient stone granite ramparts, battlements and turrets.

Built during the reign of Elizabeth I, as one of innumerable measures to protect England from the constant threat from France or Spain, or both at the same time, Portsmouth Prison was, in effect, a 16th century castle built on the very edge of Britain's south coast, with commanding views over the Solent and the Isle of Wight beyond.

The prison had been through various changes of use since its Elizabethan origins, serving as Edward VII's yacht club during the latter part of the 19th Century, and a military mental asylum for high-ranking officers during both World Wars. However, it had become famous, or at least infamous, when it opened as a finishing school for girls in 1957. By that time the castle had fallen into such a state of neglect that the school was forced to rely on the many well-rehearsed services of its nubile young pupils to fund the on-going cost of structural repair. But after every member of Ben Dillonson's Labour Party Cabinet had been filmed by one of them during one of their rather avant-garde summer parties in 1961, the school was forced to close down.

It wasn't until the United Kingdom joined the European Union in 1973 that it became a prison. What with the sudden expanse of Euro-Legislation, along with the millions of Europeans crossing the Channel unencumbered by the need of either a British passport or a rudimentary understanding of what the word *legal* meant, the burgeoning prison service could hardly keep up. Subsequently the castle was bought by Her Majesty's Government in 1979, and it has been keeping southern-based miscreants locked safely away ever since.

'Can you see a doorbell anywhere?' asked Capstan. He'd never visited Portsmouth Prison before, or any other, and simply had no idea how to gain access.

'I thought there would have been someone to let us in, Sir,' said Dewbush, 'like a Beefeater, or one of those soldiers with the tall fuzzy black hats.'

'You're thinking of the Tower of London,' responded Capstan.

'Shall we try waving our arms about, Sir, to attract someone's attention?'

'I'd rather not, if it's all the same to you.'

'How about we Google their phone number, Sir?'

'I suppose we don't have much choice. Oh, hold on. There's an intercom thing here,' and Capstan gave the grubby white plastic button a firm push.

A few moments later a metallic sounding voice came back in response.

'Who is it?'

'It's, er, Detective Inspector Capstan here from the Solent Police, oh, and er, Sergeant Dewbush.'

'And what the fuck do you want?'

'Er, we'd like to come in to talk to the person in charge, please?'

There was a pause from the other end, then the same voice came back with, *'Hold on,'* before the intercom fell silent again.

'They don't sound particularly friendly, Sir,' said Dewbush. 'I don't suppose we could negotiate with them from out here?'

'I must admit that I was thinking the same thing, Dewbush.'

Time passed. Nothing seemed to be happening. Capstan and Dewbush continued to peer over at the prison, looking and listening for any signs of life; but there were none. The only movement came from a seagull pacing up and down the fence above them, and the only sound was that of the occasional dog barking from somewhere behind them.

'Did you hear that, Sir?'

'Did I hear what, Sergeant?'

'That dog, Sir?'

'Which one?'

They both looked around, listening, until another bark echoed from somewhere far off in the distance.

'That one, Sir?'

'Yes. What about it?'

'Do you think it could be Pencil Case, Sir?'

'I really have no idea, Dewbush. They all sound the same to me.'

'Really, Sir?'

Capstan sighed. He wasn't in the mood to start engaging Dewbush in an intelligent conversation, probably because it wouldn't be, and was now undecided as to whether he'd be better off inside the prison than standing outside it; and with that at the forefront of his mind he pressed the intercom button again.

'Hello?' came a more cheerful-sounding voice.

'It's Detective Inspector Capstan and Sergeant Dewbush from the Solent Police.'

'Oh, hello,' came the reply. *'How can I help?'*

'Um,' said Capstan. 'We actually just spoke to someone a few minutes ago. They said that they'd get whoever it is who's in charge.'

'That will be Morose. Wait there, I'll see if I can find him for you,' and the intercom fell silent again.

'Did he say "Morose", Sir?' asked Dewbush, sounding even more perplexed than normal.

Capstan was also a little baffled. He too thought the person had said "Morose", but the intercom was clearly very old, and it was more likely that they'd simply misheard it, so he said, 'I think it's unlikely, Dewbush. It probably just sounded like "Morose".'

Minutes dragged by again, during which Dewbush continued to listen out for Pencil Case, secretly hoping that if the sound came a little closer it might give him a good excuse for not having to enter a prison that had recently been taken over by the entire local population of thieving, murdering miscreants who'd probably stop at nothing to steal his wallet or, worse still, the new iWatch his parents had given him for his birthday.

Eventually another, altogether different, voice came over the intercom.

'I understand that you'd like to speak to the person in charge?'

'That's right,' replied Capstan.

'Well, I am he.'

'And may I ask your name?' asked Capstan, although he had a peculiar feeling that he already knew it.

'Morose. And yours?'

At that, Dewbush jumped in the air like a sky-diving rabbit landing on a bouncy castle. 'Hello, Sir! It's Sergeant Dewbush! Do you remember me, Sir? I worked under you when you were our Chief Inspector.'

'Hello, Sergeant Dewbush. Yes, I remember.' There was an awkward pause that Morose clearly felt necessary to fill by asking, *'And how are you?'*

'Oh, very well, thank you, Sir!'

'That's nice,' said Morose.

Another moment passed during which neither party knew what to say, and which, again, Morose decided to break with the clever use of small-talk.

'And what are you working on at the moment, Sergeant Dewbush?'

'It's a special dog case, Sir.'

'A missing one?' asked Morose, remembering the days when he first started working as Chief Inspector for the Solent Police, when they had nothing better to

do than resolve arguments outside night clubs and look for missing pets.

'Yes, Sir. He's called Pencil Case, Sir. I don't suppose you've seen him around by any chance, Sir?'

'I'm sorry, I can't say that I have.'

'Oh well. Never mind. We'll just have to keep looking. Would you like to speak to Inspector Capstan, Sir?'

'Is he there?'

'He's standing right beside me, yes, Sir.' Dewbush stepped back from the intercom and looked around at Capstan. 'It's Chief Inspector Morose, Sir.'

'Yes, thank you, Dewbush. As hard as it may be to believe, I'd already managed to work that one out for myself.'

'And he'd like to speak to you, Sir,' said Dewbush, gesticulating to the yellowing plastic intercom.

Deciding that it probably was neither the time nor the place to discipline his sergeant with the usual off-the-cuff disparaging remark, Capstan simply gave his subordinate a sideways glare and, through bared teeth, said, 'Thank you, as always, Sergeant Dewbush. Very much appreciated,' whilst muttering under his breath, *you moronically inept, muppet-brained, hydraulically operated fuck-wit.* 'Good afternoon, Morose, Sir. It's Capstan here. I understand that there's been a bit of trouble inside the, er, um, where you are now, Sir.'

'I suppose that depends on your definition of a bit of trouble.'

'Are you all right, Sir?'

'Yes, perfectly all right, thank you, Capstan.'

'So, am I to understand that you have the situation under control, Sir?'

'More or less,' replied Morose.

'And is there anything we can do to help?'

'As a matter of fact there is.'

'Okay, go ahead, Sir.'

'I'd like to order some pizza.'

'Right you are, Sir,' and leaning away from the intercom Capstan said to Dewbush, 'You'd better make a note of what he wants, Sergeant.'

'Yes, Sir,' replied Dewbush, who placed his Waitrose bag down against the security fence, pulled out his notepad and pen, and said, 'I'm ready to take your order, Sir. What sort of pizza would you like?'

'Pepperoni,' replied Morose.

'And how many would you like, Sir?'

'One hundred and forty-two.'

As Dewbush wrote that down, he asked, 'Would you like anything to go with that, Sir? Garlic bread perhaps, or maybe something to drink?'

He'd had a student summer job at Offcuts Pizza back in Bath, so taking down the order came quite naturally to him.

'No, just the pizza will be fine, thank you.' As an afterthought, he added, *'How long do you think it will take?'*

'I'm not sure,' replied Dewbush, looking up at his boss.

'It's quite a big order, Sir,' said Capstan to Morose, 'So I think it's best if we pop back to the station to get authorisation before we place it. Maybe an hour? Can you wait that long, Sir?'

'I suppose we don't have much choice,' came Morose's morose reply. *'But can you be as quick as you can, else things*

could turn ugly.'

'Right you are, Sir,' said Capstan, and for lack of any other way to end the conversation said, 'Bye for now, Sir.'

'Yes, bye for now, Capstan.'

'Goodbye from me as well!' interjected Dewbush, but Morose had already gone.

'C'mon Dewbush. We'd better get back to the station, and sharpish!'

Retrieving his Waitrose bag, Dewbush stood up and said, 'I forgot to give him his grapes, Sir!'

'No time for that now, Sergeant. It will have to wait until we have the pizza.'

They made their way back to the prison car park to find their car, and narrowly missing a large white van with a huge satellite dish on its roof, they drove out to begin a time-bending, rubber-melting, ear-bleeding trip back to HQ.

Chapter Seven
The early bird

14:29 BST

WALKING STRAIGHT in through Solent Police's main entrance, Capstan saw Chief Inspector Chupples leaning up against the reception desk in the almost empty lobby. He was chatting to the Duty Officer, as they occasionally glanced up at the large widescreen TV mounted onto the wall above five blue plastic chairs, all of which were empty apart from one that had an old woman in it with a cat basket on her lap, who was either asleep, or dead; from where Capstan stood, it was difficult to tell.

'Ah, there you are, Capstan. What's the news from Portsmouth Prison?'

With a confident swagger, hindered only by his permanent need for a walking stick, Capstan replied, 'Everything's in hand, Sir.'

'That's a relief,' responded Chupples, who returned to gazing up at the TV that was showing BBC News 24, but without the sound. 'It would seem that every other prison up and down the country has had some sort of criminal uprising.'

'Really, Sir?'

'Yes. It's all over the news, and it's making all the other constabularies look a little foolish,' he said, with a gleeful little smile. 'So, it looks like our swift, decisive action saved the day for the Solent Police!'

'I suppose it did, Sir.'

'The early bird caught the worm, so to speak,' added Chupples, looking around at everyone and hoping for some sort of a congratulatory remark. But none was forthcoming, so he went on, 'We struck whilst the iron was hot!'

Dewbush thought he'd contribute to the conversation by adding, 'The rolling stone gathered no moss, Sir.'

Chupples gave him a peculiar look, which Dewbush couldn't decide was of rebuke or active encouragement, but reaching the conclusion that it must have been the latter, continued, 'Too many cooks *didn't* spoil the broth, Sir.'

'I'm sorry, Sergeant,' said Chupples, 'I'm really not with you.'

'A friend in need *was* a friend indeed, Sir. A change was as good as a rest. A penny saved was a penny earned. A miss was as good as a mile. Two in the hand was worth one in the bush. A stitch in time saved quite a lot. A nod was as good as a wink to a blind man's dog.' He couldn't think of any more after that, so stopped there and just grinned at the Chief Inspector.

'Sergeant, what on earth are you going on about?'

'Oh, sorry, Sir. I thought we were seeing how many proverbial phrases we could come up with in relation to our recent good fortune, Sir.'

Before Chupples had a chance to demote him back down to police constable for what he could only assume was taking the piss, they were interrupted by the Duty Sergeant who'd been keeping an eye on the television that was now showing the local news.

'Chief Inspector, Sir?' he said. 'You may want to see this.'

'See what?' Chupples gave Dewbush a final questioning look before glancing over at the Duty Sergeant.

'It's Portsmouth Prison. It's on the news, Sir.' He nodded towards the TV.

Frowning at the screen, Chupples said, 'I thought I told you to keep the media out of it, Capstan?'

'They must have slipped past when we weren't looking, Sir.'

'Who's that?' asked Chupples, pointing.

'That's Abigail Love, Sir,' replied the Duty Sergeant, who spent a considerable amount of his day watching the news from behind the lobby's desk. 'She's from that new local news channel, Hampshire Today, Sir.'

'Not her. That giant-sized monster of a man standing behind her.'

'I'm not sure, Sir, but he does look…familiar.'

They were all thinking the same thing.

'Well, turn it up, man. Turn it up!' said Chupples, with obvious consternation.

The Duty Sergeant obliged, and the four of them fell silent as they started to listen.

'So, can you tell me what it is you hope to achieve by taking over the prison?' the woman asked, holding the microphone up as high as she could for the enormous man to answer.

'I've already told the police what our demands are,' he said, clearly not inclined to be very helpful.

'And what are they?' the reporter prompted.

'Well, if you must know, we want pizza.'

'Pizza?'

'That's right.'

'Is that all?'

'Uh-huh.'

'So, you've taken over the entire prison and are holding twenty nine prison guards hostage, just because you want some pizza?' she asked, a little surprised.

'And if it's not here by exactly three o'clock this afternoon,' continued the unusually large man, *'we're going to kill one hostage for every minute that it's late.'*

'So if it doesn't arrive on time, you're going to execute all the hostages?' clarified the reporter, for dramatic effect.

'That's correct!'

'Well, you must all really like pizza then,' she said, and with a sweet, home-baked sort of smile, turned back to look at the camera.

'This is Abigail Love, reporting from Portsmouth Prison, hoping for the sake of the hostages and all their loved ones that the pizza isn't late.'

The Duty Sergeant hit the mute button as the Chief Inspector slowly turned around to glare at Capstan, who decided that it was a good time to straighten his tie.

Standing quietly beside him, Dewbush gave Capstan a nudge, and asked, 'Do you think that was Morose, Sir?'

'I believe it was,' replied Capstan, trying hard not to engage eye-contact with Chupples, who continued to stare directly at him.

'He's got even less hair than I remember,' remarked

Dewbush.

'He must have shaved it,' answered Capstan.

'I think he's also growing a beard, Sir.'

'Yes, I think you're right, Dewbush.'

'And he's not wearing a shirt!'

'Well, it certainly is rather hot today.'

'Never mind all that!' interrupted Chupples, still glowering at Capstan. 'I thought you said the situation was under control?'

'Sorry, Sir, but I thought it was, Sir.'

'And what on earth gave you that idea?'

'Because Morose said it was, Sir.'

'You mean Morose, as in the recently convicted mass-murdering Morose, otherwise known as The Psychotic Killer of Solent and the South Coast, the one who reportedly strangled the Prison Warden with his bare hands this morning, on the very first day of his forty-two back-to-back life sentences? That Morose?'

'Er, yes. Him, Sir.'

Chupples continued to glare at Capstan for another few moments before asking, 'Have you at least ordered the pizza?'

'Not yet, Sir. No.'

'And why the hell not?'

'We thought we'd better come back to get authorisation first, Sir.'

'You drove all the way back here to ask me for permission to buy some pizza?'

'Yes, Sir.'

'Despite the fact that if it's late, they'll start executing all the hostages?'

'Well, yes, Sir. But he didn't mention anything about killing the hostages when we were taking his order, Sir.'

Another pause followed. Chupples continued to regard Capstan as though he was some sort of prehistoric fish who'd only just crawled out of the primordial swamp, which was why he needed the stick to help keep him upright.

'So anyway,' said Capstan, 'do we have your permission to order the pizza, Sir?'

After a contemplative pause, Chupples asked, 'How many do they want?'

'I can't remember, Sir. Dewbush?'

'Oh, er, hold on.' Dewbush pulled out his notebook and began flicking through its pages to find the right one. 'One hundred and forty-two,' he eventually answered.

'Really. That many?' asked Chupples, as he reflected on his limited operational budget.

'Yes, Sir. And all pepperoni,' said Dewbush, closing his notebook.

'I see. And when do they want it by?'

Dewbush re-opened the book and flicked through it again, but couldn't find a note of the expected delivery time.

From behind them, the Duty Sergeant helped out by saying, 'The guy on the TV said that it had to be there by three o'clock, Sir.'

Chupples looked down at his watch.

'Well, it's gone half-two already. Look, you'd better just place the order. I'm sure the Commissioner won't mind, and if he does moan about it then we'll just have to take it out of your salary, won't we Capstan?'

Capstan didn't answer; but if Chupples did any such thing, then he'd be bringing the matter to the attention of both UNISON and the Police Federation.

'Well, jump to it then, or would you like a cup of tea and a cream bun beforehand?'

'I wouldn't mind a cup of tea,' said Dewbush, who'd not had one since breakfast.

Chupples gave him a very hard stare.

'C'mon Dewbush, we'd better get upstairs and place that order. We can have some tea afterwards.' Capstan led him away to begin searching for a suitable pizzeria that did bulk orders along with free delivery.

Chapter Eight
The restaurant at the top of Number 10

14:34 BST

'THIS IS NICE, isn't it,' said Robert, more loudly than usual as he guided Claire over to an empty table in the middle of the new Number10 Downing Street's rooftop restaurant.

'It's a bit breezy,' she said, endeavouring to keep control of her mass of auburn hair, as well as her light and virtually transparent summer dress, which kept trying to blow up to show everyone her perfectly formed bare bum. She was attracting enough attention as it was without exposing that particular part of her anatomy.

'A little, perhaps,' admitted Robert, 'but the view from up here more than makes up for it.'

As a waiter battled a strong head wind to pull out one of the chairs for Claire, she said, 'I suppose you can keep an eye on your golf course from up here.'

'Oh, I'm sure I couldn't see it from Canary Wharf, not without a telescope, at least,' replied Robert, as he sat down opposite her, reaching out for the drinks menu. 'It's in Kent, you know.'

'Yes, I know,' said Claire, rolling her eyes. It was the

only thing he ever talked about when he visited the family at Christmas.

'May I get you something to drink?' asked the waiter, as he attempted to hand out two wine menus without them blowing away whilst at the same time trying to prevent the pristine white tea towel that rested over his arm from flicking painfully at his face.

'What would you like, Claire? My treat.'

'Just a glass of white wine would be fine, thank you.'

'Which one would you recommend?' asked Robert, glancing up at the waiter.

'The *Coche-Dury Corton-Charlemagne Grand Cru* is proving to be very popular today, Sir.'

'I think we'll have the *Domaine Leflaive Batard Montrachet*,' said Robert, closing the menu and handing it back to the waiter.

'Yes, Sir,' he answered, and dipped his head in humble servitude.

Taking Robert's menu, and then Claire's, he tucked them securely under his arm, flattened his hair and turned away to head back down wind, weaving through the many ministerially-crowded tables to try and find a bottle of *Domaine Leflaive Batard Montrachet* from within the numerous half-unpacked tea chests that still littered all forty-two floors of the new Number 10 Downing Street.

Barging past him, the Prime Minister's Private Secretary, Fredrick Overtoun, was headed in the opposite direction.

As he approached, he said, 'Prime Minister,' more loudly than he normally would have done, by way of both introduction and apology for interrupting their meal.

'You do know that it's my lunch break, don't you Fredrick?'

'Yes, Prime Minister, it's just—'

'It's just what? That you've nobody to have lunch with and you're lonely?'

'Not exactly, Prime Minister.'

'Or did you forget your dinner money and you're hoping we'll have some leftovers?'

'Again, no, Prime Minister.'

'Well, I suggest you sod off back to wherever it was that you came from, then!'

'I'm sorry, Prime Minister, but there have been one or two recent developments that you really need to be made aware of.'

'Can't they wait?'

'Probably not, Prime Minister.'

'Oh, go one then. But this better be good.'

'Yes, Prime Minister.'

'Well?'

'Firstly, Prime Minister, we've learnt that Scotland had another independence referendum last night, and the results have come in.'

'I assume they've decided to leave us?'

'I'm afraid so, Prime Minister.'

'And good riddance to them.' There was a moment's pause. 'Was that it?'

'Er, not quite, Prime Minister. Wales also had one, and they've decided to become independent as well. Also,' continued Fredrick, as he pulled a notebook from his inside suit pocket, 'Northern Ireland's results came through, and they'll be joining them, along with Jersey, Guernsey, Gibraltar, the Falkland Islands, Anguilla, Bermuda, the British Virgin Islands, Montserrat, the Cayman Islands, Pitcairn Islands, Akrotiri and Dhekelia, Saint Helena, Ascension and Tristan da Cunha, South Georgia, and the Turks and Caicos Islands, Prime Minister.'

'To be honest, Fredrick, I haven't even heard of most of them, so I hardly think it matters, does it?'

'Oh, and the Isle of Wight as well, Prime Minister.'

'The Isle of Wight?'

'Yes, Prime Minister. They wanted to remain in the EU so they've decided to become independent and are already in the process of forming their own government.'

'Oh, well. They'll all still be part of the Commonwealth, so at least the Queen can't complain. Now, may I get back to my lunch, Fredrick, or are there any more fascinating items of news you'd like to share with me?'

'Just a couple more things, Prime Minister.'

Robert let out an audible sigh, giving Fredrick permission to continue.

'It would seem that Britain's entire European population have voted to go on strike over our decision to leave the EU, and they've just started a march through London in protest, Prime Minister.'

'Them and the rest of the country,' said Robert. 'I'm surprised there's enough room,' and he raised an amused eyebrow towards Claire.

'And finally, Prime Minister, every prison in the United Kingdom has been taken over by the inmates, and they're holding the nation's prison staff hostage.'

'And what do they want? Access to Sky Sports High Definition Premium Channels, I suppose?'

'No, Prime Minister. They're demanding pizza.'

'I can't say I blame them. I wouldn't mind something to eat myself,' he said, trying to look round his Private Secretary for any sign of the waiter.

'And they're saying that they'll start executing all the hostages if they don't get it by three o'clock this afternoon, Prime Minister.'

'Well, just give them their bloody pizza then, Fredrick. I really can't see what the problem is!'

'Unfortunately, we can't, Prime Minister?'

'And why on earth not?'

'Because Italy's part of the European Union, Prime Minister.'

'Sorry, I'm not with you.'

'They're all out on strike, Prime Minister, which means that every pizzeria the length and breadth of the United Kingdom has been closed for the day.'

Robert placed both his elbows on the table and rested his head on his hands.

'Do you have any instructions, Prime Minister?' asked Fredrick, making a deliberate point of looking at his watch. 'It's gone half-past two already.'

'Did they say what sort of pizza they wanted?' asked Claire, who'd been quietly listening to their conversation whilst playing with her still empty wine glass.

'Only that it has to be pepperoni,' answered Fredrick.

On hearing that she sat up, saying, 'May I make a

suggestion?'

'By all means,' said Robert, who'd noticed that his cutlery wasn't lined up correctly, and began making incremental adjustments so that it was.

'Well,' she said, 'if they haven't specified exactly what sort they'd like, apart from pepperoni, then couldn't you just pick up some frozen pizza from Safebusy's?'

Robert and Fredrick stared over at her. It was a very obvious solution, but as neither of them had thought of it, nor had anyone else within the nation's police force who'd all been frantically phoning every pizzeria in the entire UK to only be met with an answerphone, it was an idea of pure, innovative genius.

Not feeling the need to add anything, Robert simply looked up at Fredrick.

'I'll start making some calls now, Prime Minister,' he said, 'but before I go, should I arrange for an Emergency Meeting of the Cabinet to discuss this, and all the other matters, Prime Minister?'

'If you must. But not until after my lunchbreak. And I want Claire to sit in.'

'I'm sorry, Prime Minister, but it's against Parliamentary procedure for a non-Cabinet member to sit in on a Cabinet meeting, Prime Minister.'

'Frankly, Fredrick, as it's fairly obvious that she's the only one here who's got half a brain, I don't give a shit. Either she's in, or I'm off to play golf.'

'If you say so, Prime Minister.'

'Yes, I do say so, thank you very much. Now, off you pop, there's a good chap,' said Robert, and Claire and he watched Fredrick take one step back, turn round, and float away, like a ghost in a pinstriped suit, late for a meeting with Mr Death's Personal Assistant.

Chapter Nine
Sermon on the mount

15:17 BST

HAVING ENJOYED a delicious three course meal consisting of a starter of wild mushrooms, poached egg and a herb dressing on brioche, a main course of Gressingham duck terrine with sliced smoked chicken breast, salad of cauliflower, plum chutney and crispy bread, and a chocolate and hazelnut brownie dessert with raspberry coulis and clotted cream, all washed down with the *Domaine Leflaive Batard Montrachet,* Robert breezed into the already full Cabinet office located on the floor below his. Right behind him followed an unusually nervous Claire, whose confidence was being artificially bolstered by the two-and-a-half generous glasses of vintage wine she'd very much enjoyed during their late rooftop lunch.

'I apologise for our tardiness,' said Robert, supressing a belch, as his Cabinet rose to meet him with a variety of lopsided smiles. They all tried really hard *not* to stare directly at Claire, and all the way through her virtually transparent summer dress.

Following their gaze, Robert said, 'Oh, yes. Of course! I'd like you all to meet my brand new Marketing and Public Relations Consultant,' and he stood to one side to make sure they could all have a clear, unobstructed view of her before announcing with a proud, paternal smile, 'My niece, Claire Bridlestock!'

The Cabinet Ministers had already been advised by the PM's Private Secretary, Frederick Overtoun, that his niece would be in attendance, and had intended to mount a formal objection the moment she dared enter the Cabinet office; but on being presented with her in the flesh, most of which was on display, and being that they were all middle aged men with on-going marital problems, only lolloping tongues and bulging trousers were being put forward by way of protest.

'And I'd like her to sit next to me,' continued Robert, 'so Gerald, you can go and stand in the corner.'

'Oh, er, yes, of course,' muttered Gerald Frackenburger, the Defence Minister, adding, 'sorry,' for good measure. He held his chair out for Claire and offered her his own rather interesting version of a charming smile, that would have sent the world's horniest housewife screaming into the nearest kitchen to select a suitably sharp carving knife in a decent self-defence initiative.

'Thank you,' said Claire, whose own smile had quite the opposite effect, and as Gerald's knees buckled underneath him he blushed, rather noticeably, and took a few steps backwards in a forlorn bid to blend in with the bare white wall behind him.

As Claire sat down to Robert's right, the PM took his seat at the brand new opaque glass boardroom table, signalling the remaining Cabinet Ministers to do the same.

After giving Claire a formal nod of acknowledgment, Robert glanced around at his Ministers, whose faces all looked as if they were about to collapse under the immense weight of their own self-importance. 'So, who wants to go first?'

At these words, they all decided to do what they always did when being asked an open question, and began examining whatever it was that just happened to be on the desk directly in front of them.

'Anyone?' prompted Robert.

With still no response, Robert thought he'd better ask something a little more direct.

'What's the current situation with those prisoners?' he asked, staring at Harold Percy-Blakemore, the Home Secretary, sitting to his immediate left, opposite Claire. 'I assume that someone *was* able to get them those Safebusy's frozen pizzas, as Claire here so pragmatically suggested?'

As Claire went a little pink around the edges herself, Harold replied, 'Er, I think so, yes, Prime Minister.'

'Well, that's one problem solved then, isn't it!' and Robert beamed at everyone around the table.

'Almost, Prime Minister, but now they're demanding that they all get *Cornettos* for dessert.'

'Then give them bloody *Cornettos*! C'mon people. This really isn't that difficult!'

'We would, Prime Minister, of course, but regrettably they want the new *Cookies'n'Cream* ones, and Safebusy's don't have enough in stock to supply the nation's eighty thousand prison population, Prime Minister.'

'Then I suggest you find something else to negotiate with!'

'I suppose we could see if they'd like a *Viennartar* instead?' proposed Harold, as he looked up at Robert for approval. 'Apparently they come on a stick these days!'

'You see, Harold, you do still have full use of your brain - well, half of it at least. Well done!'

'Yes, Prime Minister, and thank you, Prime Minister,' he said, picking up his Bic biro to draw a line through *Cookies'n'Cream Cornetto* to write *Viennartar* in its place.

'Right! Good! Now, may we move on to the main item on the agenda, that of the sudden and altogether unexpected decline of my previously unprecedented popularity, and what we can do about it.'

With the exception of Claire, and Gerald Frackenburger who still stood in the corner, grateful to be out of the fray, everyone else in the room resumed their close observation of pens, or glasses of water, or blank pieces of A4 paper.

'Any ideas?' asked Robert.

There was one rather obvious solution that would instantaneously resolve the Prime Minister's on-going popularity problem, and that of the Party, but nobody was prepared to ask for his immediate and unconditional resignation, not to his face at any rate.

'One of you must have at least one suggestion,' said Robert, trying to catch someone's eye.

A tiny hand was tentatively raised from the far left hand corner of the long glass table. It was little Tom Thumberland, The Minister of Trade and Industry.

'Yes, Tom! You have an idea.'

'Er, well, Prime Minister. I thought that maybe you could, er, perhaps, um, start using a bicycle instead of a car, Prime Minister?'

'Okay, well, I don't have a bike, but it's a thought, at least. Anyone else?'

'Maybe you could use the tube instead, Prime Minister,' suggested Francis Keynes, the Minister for Transport. 'It's what Ken Livingstone used to do and it always went down well with the public.'

'If you're a militant, underground, left-wing socialist then it probably would, but as I'm not, it won't, now will it?'

'The DLR actually goes over-ground, Prime Minister, if that makes any difference.'

'Not really,' said Robert. 'Anything else?'

'You could always use the bus,' continued Francis, whose only function as Minister of Transport was to encourage as many people as possible to use either a train or a bus.

'Any ideas that don't involve alternative means of getting about?'

'You could get a dog, Prime Minister,' suggested Frank Herringbone, the Minister for Environment, Food and Rural Affairs.

'And why on earth would getting a dog make me more popular?' asked Robert.

'We conducted a survey last year that found that eight out of ten people preferred dog owners over non-dog owners, Prime Minister.'

'Is that so?' asked Robert, not sounding particularly convinced.

'Well, yes, but in fairness we did only ask other dog owners, so the results weren't as accurate as we'd have liked.'

'Really?' Robert said, with deliberate sarcasm.

Not picking up on it, Frank continued, 'Yes, Prime Minister, but as the survey was sponsored by Paxter's Thoroughbred Chump, we didn't feel we had much choice.'

'That's all fascinating. No, really, Frank, it is! But as I have absolutely no intention of spending the rest of my life following a dog around Hyde Park with a plastic bag, I'd rather not.'

Robert looked around the room again and, once more, asked, 'Anyone else?'

Another hand went up, this one attached to the Minister of Culture, Media and Sport, Mark Naviguer.

'Perhaps you could go on *Celebrity Big Brother*, Prime Minister?'

'Celebrity who?'

'*Celebrity Big Brother*, Prime Minister.'

'I've literally *never* heard of that, but please, do continue.'

'It's when they put a group of celebrities together in the same house, Prime Minister, and then they're filmed so that people can watch them on TV.'

'What on earth for?'

'To see what happens, Prime Minister.'

'And what does, normally, happen?'

'After a few days they all tend to go a bit mad, Prime Minister, mainly because they're locked up together whilst being deprived of various life essentials like food, alcohol and internet access, so it does become rather entertaining.'

'It sounds like some sort of subversive 1950s Soviet Union social experiment. I thought the general idea of living within a free Western society like ours was *not* to spend your life being locked up.'

'I think people do it because they want to be on TV, Prime Minister.'

'And how do they get out? Good behaviour, I suppose?'

'Sort of, Prime Minister. The general public votes for who they'd like to leave and every Friday someone gets evicted.'

Robert didn't look even the slightest bit convinced, so Mark added, 'It may sound a little odd, Prime Minister, but it's remarkably popular, especially amongst people who like voting for things, which is why I thought it might work rather well for us.'

'Okay. It's a possibility, I suppose, but it sounds like I'd need to be popular first, and so therefore it's probably of little help at the moment.'

'Maybe you should go on *Celebrity Bake Off* beforehand, Prime Minister?' suggested Mark, again.

'And you think that would make me more endearing in the public eye?'

'It would if you could create an impressive Victoria Sandwich Cake, Prime Minister.'

'I doubt I could, but I could have a go at making a cheese sandwich?'

'How about an Arctic Roll, Prime Minister?'

'An Arctic what?'

'An Artic Roll, Prime Minister. It's like a Swiss Roll but with ice cream, instead of jam.'

'It sounds more like what an Eskimo's dog would do, but anyway, now that I've had a chance to think about it, I hate cooking, so it's a no!' He gazed around the table once more. 'Any other ideas?'

'There's another programme called *Secret Millionaire*, Prime Minister,' continued Mark. 'It's where rich people pretend not to be, and then hang out with other people, who aren't, Prime Minister.'

'You mean I'd have to interact with poor people?'

'Yes, Prime Minister.'

'On purpose?'

'Correct again, Prime Minister.'

'Okay. That's the worst idea so far, and by a long way! Does anyone have any suggestions that don't involve using either public transport, following a dog around with a plastic bag, being locked up, baking cakes or deliberately hanging around with the poor?'

Mark put his hand up again.

Ignoring him, Robert said, 'Someone else, please?'

With an obvious cough, Mark lifted his hand a little higher, and as no one else was willing to volunteer a suggestion, Robert said, 'Go on then, but this better be good!'

'You could become an avid football supporter, Prime Minister. *Everyone* likes football, and so people would feel more like you're one of them if you did.'

'Yes, but assuming that would mean I'd have to actually watch the game, again it's a no!'

'I've already thought of that,' said Mark, with unwavering enthusiasm. 'We could simply say that you really like football, and you could then just wear an Arsenal scarf whenever you hold a press conference,

Prime Minister.'

'It's a possibility, I suppose.'

'Of course, it would be even better if you actually started to play the game. And then we could push for you to play for England. Apparently, they're desperate for players at the moment. And if, somehow, we could get you to score the winning goal during a World Cup qualifier, maybe by having it bounce off your head, then you'd become the most popular Prime Minister since Winston Churchill, Prime Minister!'

Robert gave him one of his patented hard stares, but Mark's patriotic enthusiasm for thinking up innovative ideas to help his Prime Minister become more endearing to his voting public was infectious, and soon others around the table began coming up with their own.

'You could become a Fireman for a day, Prime Minister,' proposed the Health Secretary, Lincoln Fraserhall. 'We could then arrange for you to save a baby's life, and give it a kiss outside a burning building. Newspapers love that sort of thing.'

'How about becoming a Gay Icon, Prime Minister?' suggested the Foreign Secretary, Edward de la Balles, known for his tight-fitting trousers. 'You'd then get the women's vote *and* a fair few men as well!'

'Maybe you could have a go at Stand-Up Comedy?' proposed Mark, who'd started to write some of these ideas down, and looking up from his notes, added, 'Everyone likes someone who can tell a few jokes, Prime Minister.'

Sitting on the middle right of the table, the Chancellor of the Exchequer, Gordon Sorrelton, raised his hand. 'Perhaps we could arrange for you to win an Olympic Gold Medal, Prime Minister?' Having spent the majority of his adult life thinking about gold, and how to acquire as much of it as humanly possible, he was surprised he hadn't thought of it before.

That gave Mark yet another idea. 'Maybe you could break a World Record, Prime Minister, by jumping over a bus, or something?'

'Perhaps you could go into Space, Prime Minister,' proposed Francis Keynes. 'The public always seem to like people who become astronauts.'

'You could even walk on the moon, Prime Minister,' suggested Mark.

'Maybe you could become the very first man to walk on Mars, Prime Minister,' added Francis.

Mark put his hand up again, and without waiting for permission to speak, said, 'You could go on a pub tour around Britain and buy everyone a drink as you go.'

'Yes! And then you could get beaten up outside one of them,' interjected Francis. 'People always feel sorry for someone who gets their head kicked in for no obvious reason.'

'You could discover a cure for something,' volunteered Lincoln Fraserhall. 'Like Pigeon Flu, or Vegetarian's Disease!' Then he sat bolt upright and said, 'I know! You could heal a leper, like Jesus did!' as if it was the best idea he'd ever had in his entire life.

'I don't think lepers exist anymore,' said Mark.

With unusual single-minded persistence, Lincoln added, 'You could heal someone with eczema instead! Or how about if you were assassinated, and then came back to life three days later? You could then give a speech from on top of a hill, hand out some fish fingers, heal a couple of old people with dementia and then walk on the water to your private yacht, before sailing off into the sunset, Prime Minister!'

Robert looked over at his niece and said, 'Claire, before I make this lot redundant, I don't suppose you have any slightly more sensible suggestions?'

The entire Cabinet took the opportunity to stare at her, secretly hoping that she'd suggest something really stupid that they could all laugh at.

'Um,' she said, picking up Gerald Frackenburger's pen, hoping it would give her a boost of confidence. 'Well, I, er,' she continued, and various Cabinet Ministers began elbowing each other. If she wasn't even able to come up with a complete sentence, then it would be even more hilarious. 'I suppose you could simply legalise cannabis?' she eventually said, looking up at her uncle.

The Cabinet stopped nudging each other and just sat and stared at her. Even Robert didn't know quite what to say. As the room fell into an awkward silence, Claire felt she had no choice but to back her suggestion up by adding, 'When I was at university, everyone said that you should. They even said that they'd buy you a drink if you did!'

Robert slowly looked round at his assortment of generally unattractive Cabinet Ministers, and when he'd managed to catch the eye of each and every one of them, asked, 'And *why* couldn't any of you lot have come up with that?' The Ministers renewed their examination of the items in front of them. 'Thoughts anyone? Frank?'

'Oh, er, well, um, yes, Prime Minister,' muttered the Minister for Environment, Food and Rural Affairs. 'I suspect that it probably *would* be a widely popular policy, Prime Minister.'

On the far left, Tom Thumberland's tiny hand went up again. 'If we could grow it in the UK, it would also give us something to export, Prime Minister, other than vacuum cleaners. And as we'll soon be out of the EU, there will be no legislation that could prevent us.'

'Would it be possible to grow it, here in the UK?' asked Robert.

'I don't see why not. Certainly down south. With the ongoing effects of global warming, we're already able to produce half-decent wine these days, just about.'

'Right then,' said Robert. 'I think we've found our solution. Good! So, who knows how we'd go about growing it?'

But Robert's open question was met with the usual wall of silence.

'Has anyone at least tried it before?'

Still no response, so Robert picked on the person he thought most likely to have spent his entire teenage life stoned out of his tree.

'Mark, you must have experimented with it at some stage, surely?'

'Well, s-sort of, Prime Minister,' he spluttered, 'but I never inhaled, I promise!'

At this point Claire decided to own up. She wasn't a pillar of society as everyone else in the room was supposed to be, so she didn't think it mattered.

'I smoke quite a lot when I go to music festivals,' she said. 'Especially the one held on the Isle of Wight. Apparently they grow it locally, so it's always really cheap.'

'Excellent! Thanks again, Claire. And as you're the only person here who seems to have had any actual experience, not to mention a fully functional brain, I'd like to propose that you head up this brand new initiative.'

'Don't we need to pass a Bill through Parliament to legalise it first, Prime Minister?' asked Gordon Sorrelton.

'Well, yes, I suppose. Meanwhile, I suggest that Claire here heads straight over to the Isle of Wight to do a feasibility study. You can take my helicopter. And whilst you're there, we'll make sure the Bill's pushed through both Parliament and the House of Lords. Right! Any more questions, anyone?'

Claire raised her hand.

'Yes, Claire.'

'Does this mean that I'd qualify for a pay rise?'

Chapter Ten
Would you like fries with that?

15:24 BST

HAVING SUCCESSFULLY been able to arrange for one hundred and forty-two frozen pepperoni pizzas to be delivered to Portsmouth Prison, courtesy of Safebusy's brand new "Select 'n Get" delivery service, that guaranteed arrival within just half an hour of receiving a customer's email request, Capstan and Dewbush had driven into Portsmouth town centre for a celebratory slap-up lunch, albeit rather a late one.

'Can I take your order?' asked the waitress who was chewing gum rather loudly with a finger poised over her electronic ordering tablet. As she waited for a response, she gazed at an immense flat screen TV that hung on the far side restaurant wall with a bored, vacant sort of look.

'What are you having, Dewbush?' asked Capstan.

'I'm not sure, Sir,' answered Dewbush, as they both stared at their respective menus. 'What are *you* having?'

'I'm not sure either, Dewbush.' Glancing up at the waitress, he asked, 'Excuse me, miss, but I don't suppose you have anything other than burgers?'

'Huh?'

'Sorry, but I was just wondering if you had anything other than burgers on the menu?'

Rolling her eyes, she stared down at Capstan and said, 'We've got Burger 'n Chips, Burger 'n Beans, Burger 'n Peas, Burger 'n Mash, Burger 'n Cheese, Burger 'n Bacon, Burger n' Salad or just plain Burger.'

'How about pizza?' asked Capstan, who, having spent the last couple of hours thinking about it, really fancied some.

'Look, mister, this is Bob's British Burger Bar. We only serve British food. If you want foreign stuff then you'd better go next door!'

'Yes, I see,' said Capstan, and looked down at the laminated menu before glancing back up at her again. 'I don't suppose you know if next door has re-opened yet?'

The waitress just stared back at him, unblinking, with her mouth half-open.

'Shall I have a look, Sir?' asked Dewbush.

'At what, Dewbush?'

'Next door, Sir. To see if Georgianio's is open?'

'Are you ordering or what?' asked the waitress. 'The Management don't take kindly to homeless time-wasters!'

'I'll have the Burger n' Chips, thank you,' said Capstan, handing the menu back to her with a dutiful smile.

'Would you like fries with that?' she asked, as she took the menu off him.

'Oh, er, sorry. I thought it already came with those?'

'So, that's a "no" then?' she asked.

'Well, I'd like to have chips with it, if that's what you mean?'

'Look, mister, it's quite simple. Either you want

fries or you don't!'

'Sorry, but I thought chips *were* fries.'

'If chips were fries, then they'd have the same name, now wouldn't they!' and she reverted to staring at him with her mouth open.

Somewhat confused, Capstan asked, 'Could I have fries on the side if I order the Burger 'n Salad?'

'It's your funeral,' she said, and assuming that was his order, began pressing down on various parts of her tablet's surface.

Coming to the conclusion that he'd probably been a little hasty in wanting to try Bob's British Burger Bar, which had only opened the Friday before, the day the EU referendum results had been announced, Capstan looked over at his subordinate. 'Haven't you made up your mind yet, Dewbush?'

'Can I have the Burger n'Chips, please?' he said, glancing up at the waitress.

'Would you like fries with that?' she asked.

'Oh! Um, er…' and looked over at his boss for help. Capstan just shrugged his shoulders at him, so Dewbush smiled at the waitress and said, 'Yes,' with an obvious inflexion at the end to make it sound as much like a question as possible without it actually being so.

After pressing the screen a few more times the waitress asked, 'And what do you want to drink?'

'Oh,' said Capstan, 'What do you have?'

'Tea,' she answered.

'Coffee?' asked Capstan.

She stared down at him again.

'Tea will be fine, thank you,' said Capstan. 'And my colleague will have the same.'

Retrieving the menu from Dewbush, the waitress spun around and stomped off towards the kitchen, just as a buzzing sound began to emanate from Dewbush's wrist.

'Oh, someone's calling me!' he said, clearly excited at the prospect of being able to use his new iWatch in front of his boss. 'It's Chief Inspector Chupples!' he continued, as he tapped on the green answer icon before holding it close to his mouth. 'Hello, Chief Inspector, Sir,' he replied, grinning over at Capstan.

'Who's that?' came a thin Chupplesy-sounding voice, as it echoed from the tiny speaker.

'It's Sergeant Dewbush, Sir. I'm talking to you on my brand new iWatch, Sir.'

'I'm trying to get hold of Capstan. Is he there?'

'Oh, yes, Sir. Hold on,' and he held his arm out for Capstan and said, 'It's Chief Inspector Chupples, Sir. He wants to speak to you.'

'Why couldn't he call me on my own bloody phone,' mumbled Capstan, and gave Dewbush's wrist, and the iWatch strapped to it, an odd sort of a look before leaning forward and saying, 'Capstan here!'

'Capstan! Where the hell have you been? I've been trying to call you for bloody ages!'

'We're in town, having lunch, Sir.'

'Why aren't you answering your phone?'

'I'm not sure, Sir. Hang on, let me check.' He retrieved it from inside his suit jacket pocket for a cursory examination. 'I must have forgotten to turn it on. Sorry about that, Sir.'

'Well, whilst you've been out having a jolly old time in town, we've had Portsmouth Prison on the phone, demanding that they

all get Cornettos for dessert!'

'Cornettos, Sir?'

'Yes! And not just any Cornettos, but Cookies'n'Cream ones, and the local Safebusy's don't have any! And so, in your absence, we offered them Viennartar instead.'

'Really, Sir?' asked Capstan.

'Yes, really, Sir!' replied Chupples. *'Fortunately for us they come on a stick these days, and so the prisoners accepted.'*

'That's a result then, Sir!'

'I haven't finished yet!'

'Oh, sorry, Sir. I thought you had.'

'They accepted, but on the condition that YOU were to deliver them, by hand, Capstan!'

'Who, *me*, Sir?'

'Yes, YOU, Capstan!'

'Are you sure, Sir?'

'Of course I'm bloody sure!'

'Oh! Right then, Sir.'

'It turns out,' continued Chupples, *'that the prisoner's new leader IS our former Chief Inspector after all, and he's asked for you personally, and if he doesn't get them by 3:30pm, he's going to start throwing his hostages over the prison walls!'*

'But why me, Sir?'

'WELL, I DON'T BLOODY KNOW!' shouted Chupples, clearly feeling somewhat stressed by the situation. But after a moment's pause he regained his composure and continued, *'So, anyway, we have one hundred and forty-two Viennartar ice creams waiting here for you to pick up and deliver in time to save the lives of twenty nine prison guards; and you're out, having lunch!'*

'Er, Inspector, Sir,' interrupted Dewbush, who'd just started to gaze over at the TV on the far wall that seemed to hold everyone else in the restaurant transfixed.

Ignoring him, Capstan continued his conversation with Chupples, via Dewbush's iWatch.

'So, what's the situation now, Sir?'

The situation now, Capstan, is that Morose has lined up every single one of his hostages along the top of the prison's battlements with the explicit intention of pushing them over IF the Viennartars don't arrive on time.'

'I see,' said Capstan. 'And what time is it now, Sir?'

Dewbush leaned forward and whispered with some urgency, 'Sir!' again, in a seemingly desperate bid to garner his boss's attention.

'I make it exactly 3:31pm,' answered Chupples, and a loud collective gasp went up from what must have been the whole of the restaurant's clientele.

'Sir! Inspector, Sir!' said Dewbush again, using his free hand to gesticulate towards the TV.

'For Christ sake, Dewbush! What is it?'

'It's Portsmouth Prison, Sir. They've just pushed what looked like a prison guard from off the top of the wall, Sir.'

As Capstan looked up, the waitress appeared with their order.

'Burger n'Salad?' she asked.

'Oh, er, that's me,' said Capstan, looking down at the plate being laid in front of him.

'Burger n'Chips?' she asked again.

'Me, please!' said Dewbush, who gazed up at the waitress, caught her eye, smiled and said, 'Thank you very much!'

'Excuse me, miss?' asked Capstan, 'but didn't I

order the Burger with Salad?'

'Yes, and?'

'Well, it's just that I can't see any of the, er, salad?'

'It's in the burger!' she said, and pointed at it.

Capstan lifted up the bap to reveal a slice of cucumber.

'Oh yes, so it is,' said Capstan.

'Right,' continued the waitress, 'I suppose I'd better get you your teas then,' and she spun around to make her way back to the kitchens.

'Capstan? Capstan? Are you still there?' came Chupples' voice from Dewbush's iWatch.

'Oh, yes, Sir. Sorry Sir. The waitress was just giving us our food.'

'Well?'

'Well, what, Sir?'

'Are you at least going to *offer* to do something about this situation or not?'

Another gasp went up from the restaurant's clientele and Capstan turned around to look at the TV, just in time to see the second prison guard finishing off his descent. He glanced at his own watch, down at the Burger n' Salad in front of him, and pleased to see that it had come with chips after all, asked, 'Do we know exactly how many hostages they have, Sir?'

'What's that got to do with anything?'

'I think they had twenty-nine, Sir,' said Dewbush, as he continued to watch the live TV news broadcast from Portsmouth Prison.

'Well, I'm just thinking, Sir, that it will take us at least fifteen minutes to drive back down to the station to pick up the ice creams, and then another fifteen to get to the prison. So if they're going to push one prison guard over every minute, which it looks like they will, then realistically, Sir, there's probably not much point,' and he stared down at his food, trying to decide if he should eat it with his hands or be more civilised and use a knife and fork instead.

'*ARE YOU KIDDING ME?*' asked Chupples.

'Also, Sir,' interjected Dewbush, 'there are only twenty-seven left now. Oh no, hold on, make that twenty-six,' and he, Capstan, and everyone else in the restaurant watched as another guard was pushed over the wall to his certain death.

'*I'm holding you directly responsible for this, Capstan! Do you hear me?*'

'Yes, Sir. Thank you, Sir,' replied Capstan, and used one of his hands to mime cutting his own throat as a signal for Dewbush to end the call.

Pulling his arm back, Dewbush leaned in to the iWatch and said, 'Bye Sir,' before pressing the red "End Call" icon.

'I can't believe this!' said Capstan, as he lifted his bap up again. 'Since when has a "salad" been reduced to a single slice of cucumber?'

'I thought it was a gherkin?' asked Dewbush, more used to eating out at McDonald's.

'No, it's definitely a cucumber,' said Capstan, closing the bap to pick the whole thing up. 'Looks all right though,' he said with almost a smile, and shoved as much of it as he could into his mouth as the restaurant's clientele roared out another collective gasp as a fourth guard was hurled off the top of the prison battlements.

Chapter Eleven
Twenty-nine, all in a line

15:54 BST

IT WAS TURNING out to be an unusually warm, breathless afternoon, as Morose stared out through a pair of binoculars at a growing crowd of journalists beneath.

He was standing at the very top of Portsmouth Prison's ancient granite battlements, but with no shade, and without Portsmouth's normal perpetual stiff breeze, he was having to endure the full force of the British summer sun as it beat down on his recently shaved head with unrelenting single-mindedness. It had become so hot that he'd even taken his shirt off an hour or so earlier, something he'd never have considered doing in his former role as a Police Chief Inspector, not even in the privacy of his own garden.

But since becoming the head of COCK he felt almost liberated. However, despite being naked from the waist up, and standing at least fifty feet up in the open coastal air, he was still hot. He'd even go so far as to say that he was damned hot, but apart from having a deliciously refreshing ice cream, he couldn't think of anything he could do about it. So he just stood there, breathing in and out, feeling the sweat run down over the bulging fat that gently undulated beneath his skin with each laborious intake of breath.

Using one hand to wipe his forehead, he asked, 'How many guards do we have left, Bazzer?'

The question was directed at another hulk of a man standing to his immediate right wearing standard-issue prison overalls, slicked-back dark hair and a trendy-looking pair of sunglasses that he'd "borrowed" from one of the guards.

Using a single finger to count the remaining hostages, the man, who only just a few hours earlier had been one of Humpty's personal bodyguard's, replied, 'Only five, Gov.'

'And still no sign of those Viennartars?'

'Don't look like it, Gov.'

'That's another minute gone,' said an equally large man standing to Morose's left. He was the second of Humpty's paid bodyguards, who went by the name of Gazzer, cousin to Bazzer. But now that Humpty the Dumpty had had the great fall his destiny had demanded, they'd simply started to follow Morose around, in the misguided assumption that they'd still get paid to do so.

'OK,' said Morose. 'Push another over, will you please, Bazzer?'

'No probs, Gov.' With hands and feet bound, and silver gaffer tape flattened over his mouth, the twenty-fifth prison guard was shoved over the side, and he plummeted down without so much as a whimper.

They all listened for the audible gasp that emanated from the British press below each time they did so, closely followed by the usual burst of flash photography.

'Shall I count down another minute, Gov?' asked the bodyguard to Morose's left.

'If you could, Gazzer.'

'Right you are, Gov.'

'If you don't mind me sayin' so, Gov,' said Bazzer on the right, as the line of hostages were all moved up so that the next one stood directly in front of him, 'but I could really do with that ice cream.'

'Me too!' said Gazzer, without taking his eyes off his watch.

'And we seem to be runnin' low on guards.' He looked down the rapidly shrinking line of those remaining.

'Bloody Capstan,' muttered Morose, as he put the binoculars down and massaged his eyes within their sockets. 'How difficult can it be to deliver a hundred sodding ice creams?'

'Who's Capstan?' asked Bazzer.

'Never mind,' said Morose, staring back down.

'Maybe they had a puncture?' suggested Bazzer.

'Maybe they melted?' added Gazzer.

The hostage standing in front of him began nodding in agreement to both suggestions, as his eyes darted about, clearly desperate to effect some sort of escape from having to be the one to go over next.

'Is that them there, Gov?' asked Bazzer, pointing over the prison guard's head at a rapidly approaching white van.

As Morose brought his binoculars to his eyes again to train them upon the vehicle in question, all the remaining hostages stood up on their toes to have a look for themselves.

91

After a few moments, Morose said, 'I'm afraid not! It looks like it's from The Daily Mail.'

'That's another minute gone, Gov,' said Gazzer.

'Shall I push this one over?' asked Bazzer.

As the hostage started to mumble his formal objection as he frenetically shook his head, along with the rest of his body, clearly hoping that his own disapproval might have some bearing on the decision, Morose said, 'Well, as I can't see another Safebusy's delivery van, and as there's still no sign of bloody Capstan, I suppose you'd better.'

A casual shove drew a single squeak from the prison guard as he began his own rather rapid descent.

Listening to the now all-too familiar thud, Bazzer peered over the side and said, 'You'd 'ave thought they'd 'ave put something down there to break their fall by now.'

There was a pause as Gazzer also looked over at what was now an impressive pile of bodies, before asking, 'Like what?'

'Dunno. A pillow, or som'in'.'

'A pillow wouldn't be big enough,' said Gazzer, massaging his impressive angular jaw.

'Some cushions, then?'

'They could 'ave used a mattress, I 'spose,' said Gazzer. 'Or maybe some sort of 'n airbed?'

'A blow-up doll would have been good,' mused Bazzer. 'Then they'd at least 'ave had somethin' to look forward to when they got to the bottom, like,' and smirked at his own joke.

Without so much as a smile, Gazzer added, 'They could've stuck a trampoline down there.'

'Nah! They'd just 'ave bounced up again.'

'Yeah, but then we could've hit' um with som'in', before they went back down.'

'What, like a baseball bat?'

'T'spose, but I don't think we've got one.'

There was another pause before Bazzer suggested, 'We've got 'n axe though!'

Looking over at him, Gazzer asked, "Ave we?'

'Yeah! There's one in the guard's canteen. I saw it there once, next to their coffee machine. They keep it in a glass cabinet. I remembers cus there was a sign next to it that said, "In case of fire, break glass," or som'n, which I thought was odd, like.'

'How d'ya mean?'

'I couldn't work out why they'd need to break the glass of their own coffee machine, but then I realised that if there was a fire-like, and the electrics cut out, then the machine wouldn't work, and they'd need the coffee to pour out over the fire. Or they'd need a drink, cus of the heat. And that's why they'd need the axe, like.'

'Makes sense, I'spose.'

'But then I thought that was really stupid-like, cus they'd not put anything on the wall to break the glass with to get the axe.'

'What, like a hammer, or som'n?'

'Yeah. Or a baseball bat.'

'Or another axe.'

'Are you still keeping an eye on the time?' asked Morose.

'Oh, um, er... sorry, Gov. I reckon that must be about another minute. What d'ya think, Bazzer?'

'Yeah, that was another minute. Shall I push this one over, Gov?'

With an audible sigh, Morose said, 'I suppose, but it looks like we're going to have to think of another way to get some dessert.'

'That's a shame, Gov,' said Bazzer, giving the twenty-seventh prison guard a hearty shove. 'I really fancied a Viennartar.'

'Me too, Gov! I've not had one in ages, and never one on a stick before!'

'Me neither,' added Bazzer. 'I don't s'pose we could order som'in online, like, Gov'?

'Unfortunately, none of us have any credit cards.'

'But can't we use the guards'? They all had loads of 'em in their wallets!'

'We could try, I suppose,' said Morose, 'But I'd have thought the banks would have cancelled them all by now. Anyway, let's give them another couple of minutes, and just hope that the ice cream shows up.'

Chapter Twelve
Ticket to Sandown Airport, near Ryde

16:45 BST

A S THE VERY last prison guard was descending the front of Portsmouth Prison, Claire Bridlestock, the Prime Minister's niece, was flying down towards the South Coast of England in MDK Aviation's latest helicopter, the Liquidator Super X-6000, speeding ever-closer towards their destination: the Isle of Wight.

Having sat quietly for some time, and having only exchanged pleasantries with the pilot when she'd first climbed aboard, she eventually decided to break the ice, and, to counteract the noise of the blades slicing through the air directly above their heads, raised her voice to ask, 'So, how does this thing work, then?'

'What, the helicopter?' questioned the man sitting opposite her, also with more volume than normal, and giving her a sideways sort of glance.

The pilot was an exceptionally good-looking, well-proportioned man, probably in his late twenties, who, most importantly, wasn't wearing a wedding ring. The combination of being seated in such close proximity to him, and being in a helicopter for the very first time, was leaving her feeling as excited as a schoolgirl who'd just been given a battery operated hockey stick for her sixteenth birthday.

'Yes, the helicopter,' she repeated, unsure as to what else she could have meant, but not particularly surprised. From her relatively extensive experience of dealing with the opposite sex, the good-looking ones always had a tendency to be a salad short of a buffet.

The pilot took a moment or two to formulate a descriptive response that he thought would make sense to her, and after about thirty seconds of contemplative consideration, came up with, 'It's like an upside down hairdryer.'

'I see,' said Claire, reassured that his stupidity was in direct proportion to his looks. Then she pointed at what was sticking up between his legs, the thing he'd been holding on to with both hands ever since they'd taken off, almost as if his life depended on it. 'And what does *that* do?' she asked.

In order to make sure that they were on the same page before answering, he took the precaution of glancing down to where it was, exactly, that she was pointing.

'It's called a joy stick,' he answered.

'Oh,' she said, raising an eyebrow, and a moment later asked, 'I don't suppose I could hold it?'

The pilot gave her a quick double-take, glanced at the joy stick again, down at his lap, and then back at her. And as his manhood began to swell up in hedonistic expectation, he re-positioned himself in his seat.

'Would you like to?' he asked, feeling his heart pick up a beat.

He'd never been given a hand-job before, not

whilst flying at any rate, and certainly not from such a stunningly attractive young woman wearing what could only be described as a completely see-through dress.

'Yes! Very much so!' she answered, catching his eye.

But then the pilot remembered one of the first things he'd been taught when learning to fly a helicopter; that under absolutely no circumstances was he allowed to give, or receive, either a hand- or blow-job whilst flying.

Forcing that memory to the forefront of his mind, he said, 'We'd better not. I'd probably crash!' He grinned at her, adding, 'But I'll give you my number when we land.'

Without a clue as to what she'd said or done to make him think that she desperately wanted his phone number, she peered out ahead of her again. She would have liked to have had it, of course, but that was hardly the point. It was down to the girl to offer, not the guy to assume.

Having sat there for another few minutes thinking about that, she sat bolt upright and said, with some excitement, 'Is that it?'

'Is what it?'

'The Isle of Wight!'

'Is it?' he asked.

'Well, it looks like it, sort of.'

She didn't have a clue what The Isle of Wight would look like from two hundred feet up, but she did at least know what an island was, and what she was looking at was definitely one of those.

'Sorry,' said the pilot, 'but I've never been down this way before. I normally just fly around London.

Hold on, we'd better check our coordinates.'

Still staring ahead, he pulled a large AA road map out from beside his seat and handed it over to her.

'Here, have a look, will you?'

Taking the A3-sized map from his hand, she asked, 'Don't you have some sort of GPS navigation system?'

'Well, yes, we do. It's fitted with the latest heads-up display unit, but for some reason it keeps showing repeat episodes of The Antiques Road Show, which can be a little distracting. So anyway, we switched it off for now, until we can get it fixed. If you take a look at pages twenty-two and twenty-three, we should be on there somewhere.'

Opening the map to the suggested pages, Claire did her best to match what she could see out of the window with what was featured on the map.

After waiting patiently for a few minutes, the pilot asked, 'What do you think?'

'Well, from what I can make out, if that's the A27, then that down there should be Hayling Island. The Isle of Wight must be further out.'

'Oh, yes, I think I can see it now,' he said. 'Just up ahead. Okay, I'm going to call their control tower and get permission to land.' Reaching over to a dial on the dashboard's two-way radio, he began a completely different conversation.

'Sandown Airport, Sandown Airport, this is PM1 calling. Over.'

After a brief pause, a metallic-sounding voice came back.

PM1, PM1, this is Sandown Airport. Receiving you. Over.'

'Sandown Airport, this is PM1. Requesting permission to land. Over.'

'PM1, this is Sandown Airport. We have identified you on our radar, the air space is clear and we can confirm that you have permission to land. Please use the helipad marked, and may we take this opportunity to welcome you to the People's Independent Republic of the Isle of Wight. Over.'

'Roger that. Over and out.'

Claire looked over at the pilot. 'The People's Independent Republic of the Isle of Wight?'

'Apparently!' he replied. 'It must be what they've decided to call themselves since becoming independent.'

'Oh!' said Claire, her smooth, line-free forehead creased with concern. 'It all sounds very…left wing.'

'Like some sort of communist military state,' agreed the pilot. 'Anyway, I can see the helipad now, and it looks like they've rolled out the red carpet for you.'

'So it seems,' she said. 'Are those tractors?'

'Looks like it. But I think that big red one is a combine harvester. The others all look like either quad bikes, Range Rovers or Land Rover Discoverys.'

'And why are the people all wearing wellington boots with green scarfs wrapped around their heads?'

'I'm really not sure,' he said, as perplexed as she was, and they both took a moment to stare down at the awaiting group, who also seemed to be carrying a variety of gardening implements, including rakes, hoes and shovels. From where they were, now flying only about twenty feet above them, they looked like a group of French Revolutionaries getting ready to go to a Robin Hood fancy dress party.

Claire couldn't help feel a little concerned. It really wasn't what she was expecting. There was a definite look of continental insurgence about them, and there must have been two dozen down there, at least! But as she couldn't see anything that resembled a Guillotine, not in the traditional sense, she did her best to smile down at them all, occasionally adding a wave for good measure.

'Okay. I'm going to land, but after I've set it down, don't let me forget to give you my phone number.'

'You're not going to leave me there, are you?'

'Unfortunately, I have to. I need to get back to London. But give me a call at some stage and we can go out for that, er, drink,' and he turned to give her a highly suggestive wink.

With more pressing matters on her mind, other than how he'd managed to get it into his head that she'd already agreed to have sex with him, she gave him a half-smile.

'OK, but can you at least hang around long enough to make sure they don't either stick my head in a stock and throw apples at it, or cut it off to see if I'm a witch?'

'I don't think that's what you do to find out if someone's a witch,' he said, as he stabilised the controls to hover over the helipad. 'They'd be more likely to throw you into a pond to see if you sank or swam.'

'And if I sank?'

'Then they'd probably leave you to drown.'

'Oh,' said Claire.

'But if you floated,' the pilot continued, with a more

upbeat tone of voice, 'then it would be a sure sign that you *were* a witch after all, and they'd drag you out and burn you at the stake.'

'So, it's a win-win then.'

He smiled at her.

'Don't worry. I was only joking. I'm sure they'll be very nice, once you get to know them all.'

But as he began blasting the audience beneath with an all-encompassing vortex of dust and desiccated vegetation, and as the assortment of gardening tools sparkled in the sunlight, which made them look even more menacing than they did before, the less convinced he became, and he decided that he would stick around after all, for a while at least, just in case she needed a gallant rescue. The Prime Minister's personal helicopter had been installed with bulletproof glass and was fitted with two M61 multi-barrelled 20mm rotary cannons, each firing at a rate of 6,600 rounds per minute. So if they were foolish enough to mount a Market Farmer's version of an all-out assault, they'd be dolphin fodder within just a few seconds.

Chapter Thirteen
The People's Independent Republic

17:11 BST

A S THE HELICOPTER landed, and Claire fumbled with her belt buckle, a splinter group of five broke off from the main welcoming party and jogged over towards them, as best they could at any rate in their matching green wellies.

Each using at least one hand to prevent their khaki-green head scarfs from being blown off, and keeping their heads well down to avoid being either scalped or decapitated by the helicopter's blades, they made for the passenger side door. One of the five pulled it open, held out a hand and shouted, 'YOU MUST BE CLAIRE BRIDLESTOCK?'

With a nervous smile and a nod of acknowledgment, Claire called back, 'THAT'S ME!' She took the offered hand and stepped carefully down onto terra firma, only to join the others in being blasted by the blades above, leaving her no choice but to take hold of the bottom of her light summer's dress with her free hand in a desperate bid to stop it from being blown off, straight over her head. If she'd allowed that to happen, she'd have been stranded in the middle of an airfield, wearing nothing more than a pair of stilettos and a sheepish smile.

Spotting her predicament, the person who continued to hold her hand wasted no time in guiding her away from the helicopter's blades to where the main welcoming party waited, far from the threat of unceremonial decapitation and unsolicited indecency. After all, neither scenario would have played out well on the BBC's Ten O'Clock News.

Somewhat surprised to see that their distinguished visitor, the British Prime Minister's niece, was an absolute corker, and that she appeared to be wearing nothing at all but a completely transparent dress, an eager young reporter leapt to the front of the group, took to one knee and began taking a relentless series of pictures, all the while feeling himself stiffen up with unadulterated voyeuristic pleasure. The very moment he'd spotted her, and the situation she'd found herself in, he'd seen that it made no difference if her dress stayed on or blew straight off. Either way, she looked as if she was completely naked, and realising that he was set to make an absolute fortune selling the pictures to the British press, he tried desperately to capture just about as many parts of her exposed anatomy as possible.

However, the person who'd guided Claire away from the helicopter saw what he was up to and, lifting a green wellie-clad foot, booted him over, leaving him sprawled on his back. This only gave the reporter an even better view, and taking full advantage of this extraordinary new angle, shouted, 'OI, LUV! OVER HERE!'

Instinctively, Claire turned, and seeing that it was a reporter, now on his side, gave him a smile that just happened to coincide with her dress blowing up once again to reveal her naked bum and just about everything else, the combination of which gave the reporter little choice, and he had an almost instantaneous orgasm.

Breathing hard, he called out, 'Thanks, luv!' and then collapsed onto his back, rested his camera on his heaving chest and pulled out a packet of Marlboro and a lighter.

'Sorry about that,' said the person who'd guided her from the helicopter. 'It's young Joe-Bob Brown. He's always been a little over-exuberant on such occasions.'

'Oh, that's all right,' said Claire, as she was finally able to take control of her dress, smoothing it down over her body before giving her hair a quick, lifesaving sort of prod.

'Anyway, I'd like to formally welcome you to the People's Independent Republic of the Isle of Wight,' she said, and held out a hand. 'I'm Chairperson Florence.'

On the spur of the moment, Claire decided that the occasion called for a curtsy, which she did, before shaking her hand. 'How do you do?'

'And may I introduce you to the People's Secretary of Agriculture, Comrade Giles.'

'How do you do?' said Claire again, with another curtsy.

'No, how do *you* do?' asked Comrade Giles, with genuine interest.

'The People's Secretary of Estates and Agents, Comrade Jeffrey,' continued Florence.

'How do you do?' said Claire again.

'No, how do *you* do?' asked Comrade Jeffrey.

'The People's Secretary of Vehicles and Recreation, Comrade Brian.'

With a further curtsy and yet another formal handshake, Claire said, 'How do you do?'

Stepping forward, Comrade Brian also asked, 'No, how do *you* do?'

'And the People's Secretary of Sailing and Transportation, Comrade John Long-Silverton!'

'How do you do?' said Claire once more.

'No, how do *you* do?' asked Comrade John Long-Silverton, who she couldn't help but notice was very old and had a wooden leg.

'Did you lose that in the War?' she asked, feeling more royal by the minute.

'I beg your pardon, miss?' he asked, as he slowly lifted a withered hand to cup an ancient ear.

'I just wondered if you lost your leg during the War?'

'Did I?' he asked, looking down.

'Anyway,' interrupted Chairperson Florence who, with a large round head, an abundance of freckles and a tangled mop of grey hair, looked remarkably like a middle-aged version of the popular character from the 70's hit children's series, *The Magic Roundabout*. 'We're all delighted that you've been able to come to help us celebrate our very first day as an independent country.'

She ushered her away from Comrade John Long-Silverton, who'd started to pivot around on his wooden leg, muttering to himself, 'I could have sworn I had one earlier.'

'And I'd also like to apologise for our rather brash

display of military strength.'

'You mean the gardening tools?' asked Claire.

Leading her towards the nearest Land Rover Discovery, Florence continued, 'To be honest, we weren't sure what to expect from the British Government after announcing our decision to become independent this morning.'

'Oh, how come?' asked Claire, who knew her uncle wouldn't have cared less.

'Well, we were a little concerned that they may send over some sort of an armed force in a bid to take back control, so we wanted to be ready to repel borders.'

'With gardening tools?' asked Claire again.

'Not only hand-held farming implements,' continued Chairperson Florence. 'We also have a combine harvester.' As she opened the door of the Discovery for Claire to climb in, she gesticulated to the giant-sized piece of automotive farming equipment. 'It can harvest a field as big as a football pitch in just twenty minutes, so I'd hate to think what it would do to an army battalion. Anyway, hop up, my dear, and I'll give you the tour.'

Doing as she was told, Claire stepped up and began to make herself comfortable in the plush tanned leather seat. By the time she'd put her seatbelt on, Florence had made her way around to the driver's side, opened the door and heaved herself in.

'Right then!' she said. 'What would you like to see first?'

Considering that to be a sufficient cue to discuss what she'd actually come to talk about, Claire asked, 'If you don't mind, I'd quite like to see where it is that you grow your organic produce?'

Florence gave her an odd look.

'You mean, you'd like to see some of our fields?'

'Well, yes, sort of, but more a particular crop that you grow on them.'

'Like potatoes and cabbages?' asked Florence, still confused. She'd love to show Claire the fields where they grew all their vegetables, but it was certainly the first time she'd ever been asked.

Claire decided to take a risk.

'I was actually thinking more about your cannabis plantations?'

Chairperson Florence turned to stare directly at Claire's face. The Isle of Wight's cannabis farms had been a closely guarded secret which, up until that very moment, they thought they'd been able to keep from the UK mainland, so she was just a little perturbed to suddenly discover that word had somehow leaked out. But, she consoled herself, as a brand new independent country, it hardly mattered anymore; there wasn't a damned thing the British Government could do about it.

Still watching her closely, and as Claire began to distract herself from the close scrutiny by playing with some of the many and varied knobs and dials on the dashboard, Florence asked, 'May I ask if there's any particular reason *why* you'd like to see them?'

Claire turned to look back at her.

'Listen,' she said, 'I know that nobody is supposed to know about them, but I've been to a fair few of your festivals in the past and have slept, I mean *met* with a number of residents who've just happened to mentioned them during, er, whilst having, um, well…you know what I mean,' and Claire couldn't help but look more than a little embarrassed.

'I see,' said Chairperson Florence, who'd already begun to warm to the British Prime Minister's niece.

She herself wasn't born and bred on the island. She'd simply never left after attending the notorious Isle of Wight Festival held during the latter part of August, 1970, when she and 600,000 other people had rocked up to watch the likes of Jimi Hendrix, Jethro Tull, The Doors, The Who, Free, Joni Mitchell, Leonard Cohen, Kris Kristofferson and Donovan perform. It was *that* festival which had led the British Government to first view the island as a potential threat to the UK Mainland, and only a year later they'd introduced what was called the Isle of Wight Act, which limited the numbers permitted to attend such events down to only 5,000, without applying for a special licence first. Had anyone decided to put in an application for such a special licence, they'd have been turned down flat.

It wasn't until 2002 that the Isle of Wight Festivals kicked off again, and it was then that the very first talks were held to seek formal independence. But it had taken the Brexit Referendum to finally give them both the opportunity and the excuse to leave.

'And my uncle has decided to make cannabis legal in the UK,' continued Claire, 'and sent me over here to discuss some sort of a trade deal with you.'

'Right then!' said Comrade Florence, unable to supress a beaming great smile. 'I'd better take you straight over. And perhaps we can try a sample of this year's crop, to see how it's coming along. We can have a bit more of a chat about what you have in mind then.'

On those words she started the engine, shunted it into first gear and rolled the shiny black Land Rover Discovery over the airfield, up onto Embassy Way. There she shifted it into second and began heading out towards Blubber's Farm, which at just over two thousand hectares, was their largest cannabis plantation by far, and lay just the other side of the small village of Blackwater.

Chapter Fourteen
Trade talks over tea

17:38 BST

AFTER A WHISTLE-STOP tour of Blubber's Farm, Chairperson Florence drove Claire over to the estate's cottage, where The People's Independent Republic of the Isle of Wight's Secretary of Agriculture, Comrade Giles, lived. This was a quite delightful English farmhouse situated on a gentle ridge at the very end of the farm, which offered extended views over the entire plantation. With its thatched roof, white picket fence, traditional leaded windows and winding garden path surrounded on all sides by the most perfect white roses, all of which were in full bloom, it wouldn't have looked out of place on a biscuit tin, or even a 2000-piece Ravensburger jigsaw puzzle.

'Giles is probably round the back,' said Florence, unlatching the white garden gate for her.

Walking through and onto the path, Claire breathed in the warm perfumed summer air and listened to the occasional bee buzzing between flowers, along with the mellow song of a blackbird that she could hear nearby. She couldn't remember experiencing such peaceful serenity before, and could almost feel the oppressive burdens of city life lift gently from her shoulders.

'This is delightful!' she called back to Florence, who was following the Countryside Code by securing the gate behind her.

'Yes, well, Giles's garden is his pride and joy. If you keep following the path around, he'll no doubt be lurking at the back somewhere.'

When Claire had managed to circumnavigate to the rear of the cottage, she found herself on a large patio surrounded by a variety of ornate potted plants and a wooden table with four matching chairs.

Florence, rounding the corner to join her, called out, 'Hello? Giles? Are you out there somewhere?'

A head popped up from behind a shelf in a greenhouse, and it wasn't long before Comrade Giles could be seen fighting through an abundance of flora as he made his way towards them, still wearing his unusual green bandana, but apart from that looking about as much like an avid gardener as one could possibly imagine.

'Hello, Flo, and hello to you, Miss Bridlestock. Really good to see you again!' he said with a sincere smile.

'I brought Claire around to chat about our special produce.'

'Really?' asked Giles, a clear note of concern edging his voice.

'Don't worry,' continued Florence. 'She knew about it before. She's been to a few of our music festivals.'

'Ah! I see.' He laid his secateurs on the patio table and began to remove his gardening gloves.

'And there's some very interesting news from

across the Solent.'

'Oh yes. And what's that?'

'The British Government is apparently going to make it legal, and Claire's been sent over to discuss a possible trade deal.'

Setting his gloves down alongside the secateurs, he glanced at Claire and couldn't help but rub his hands together with hopeful expectation.

When they'd first sat down to discuss becoming independent from mainland Britain they'd considered that marijuana would probably become their main cash crop for export, but they'd never imagined in a million years that their very first international buyer would be the United Kingdom.

'Well, that all sounds *very* promising,' he said, as he walked around behind them, heading towards an open pair of leaded patio doors.

Poking his head half inside, he called out, 'Darling? We have visitors!' and looked back to ask, 'Would you both like a cup of tea?'

'That would be splendid, Giles!' said Florence.

'Oh, yes, please!' added Claire.

As they responded, a cheerful looking middle-aged lady with scarlet cheeks and a mass of curly red hair popped her head out of an upstairs window and called down, 'Oh, hello, everyone! Can I get you all some tea?'

'I've already asked them, darling.'

'Oh, thank you, darling. And what did they say?'

'They said that they would, darling.'

'Are you sure, darling?'

'I'm fairly sure, darling. Would you like me to ask

them again?'

'No, don't worry, darling, *I'll* do it,' and she gazed down at their two visitors and asked, 'Would you two like a nice cup of tea?'

'We both would, thank you, Margery,' answered Florence.

'Milk and sugar?'

'Just milk for me,' said Florence.

'And the same for me,' called up Claire, adding a 'thank you!' out of politeness.

'I'll pop down and get the kettle on then.' The lady's head disappeared back inside.

'So,' said Giles, turning around to face Claire again, 'they're finally going to legalise marijuana, are they?'

'It still needs to be run through Parliament and the House of Lords, but apparently that's just a formality.'

Giles stepped over and held out one of the patio chairs.

'And how much do you think they'd be looking to buy?'

Taking the seat being offered, Claire asked, 'How much do you think you'd have to sell?'

'I suppose that would depend on which type they'd want.'

'How'd you mean?'

'Well, there are three species of marijuana, and seven sub-species.'

'I'd no idea!'

'It's not exactly common knowledge,' said Giles, as he sat down himself. 'The three species are Cannabis Sativa, Cannabis Indica and Cannabis Ruderalis, but Sativa and Indica are the most popular because they contain the highest levels of Tetrahydrocannabinol, or THC as we like to call it.'

Struggling with the chemical-sounding name, Claire asked, 'And what is *Tetrahydrocannabinol* when it's at home?'

'It's the main psychoactive ingredient.'

Claire still looked confused, so Giles added, 'It's what makes you get high,' and grinned over at her. 'Cannabis Ruderalis, on the other hand,' he continued, 'does still contain THC, but in a more dilute form. But the advantages of Ruderalis, for us farmers at least, is that it's a more hardy plant, and so it's more resilient to disease and the uncertainty of the British weather. So we generally grow all three, just in case one crop fails.'

A loud clanking noise came from behind them, as Margery emerged from what must be the kitchen carrying a large silver tea tray.

'Here we are,' she said, setting it down before them. 'Now, there's the tea, and there's the marijuana. Do please help yourselves and I'll pop back for the cake.'

As Giles stood to start pouring out the tea, Claire found herself transfixed by what looked to be a fruit bowl filled to the brim with pre-ground cannabis.

Seeing what she was looking at, Giles said, 'Help yourself! It's the Sativa variety. We've been exceptionally lucky with the weather this year, so it really is rather good.'

'Oh,' said Claire, unsure as to what else to say. She'd never been offered grass during high tea before, not that she could remember at least, and in a bid to exclude herself, said, 'Unfortunately I didn't think to bring any Rizla.'

'Don't worry, my dear,' said Florence, who'd already started skinning-up a joint. 'You can share one with me.' She finished rolling one up, twisted one of its ends and placed it down on the patio table. Then she picked up her Rizla packet, tore off a small, rectangular section of card from its cover and made a makeshift filter out of it that slotted into the joint's untwisted end. Smoothing out the wrinkles between her fingers, she popped it into her mouth, pulled out a lighter from inside her green quilted waistcoat and sparked it up.

Claire watched as she inhaled and held her breath, before handing it over to her, and with a polite smile, took it from her, trying to remember the last time she'd actually had any. Realising that it must have been the previous year's Isle of Wight Festival, she took a tentative toke, inhaled a small amount, held her breath momentarily and exhaled. Delighted that she hadn't embarrassed herself by coughing all over her hosts, she repeated the process but with a little more confidence, and then passed it back to Florence.

Meanwhile, Giles had poured out the tea and passed Claire a delicate cup that rested rather precariously on a fragile-looking saucer.

'Help yourself to milk,' he said, placing a small jug beside her cup. He picked up his own tea, leant back in his chair, looked over at Claire and asked, 'So, what do you think?'

'Huh?' said Claire.

'Our latest crop?' he asked again, using the cup in his hand to point at the bowl on the table.

'Oh, that!' she said, feeling even more relaxed than she had when she'd arrived. 'Well, I'm no connoisseur or anything, but I'd have to say that it's pretty damned good!'

'Excellent!' said Giles, and then by way of making conversation, added, 'It's a remarkably popular drug, considering it's banned in just about every country around the world.'

'Apart from here, of course,' said Florence, passing the joint back to Claire.

'And the UK,' said Claire, taking it from her.

'So it would seem,' said Giles. 'It's also legal in Australia, for personal use only though, and the same in the Netherlands, of course.'

'Don't forget Columbia,' Florence said, taking a sip from her tea.

'Well, yes,' said Giles, 'But I think *everything's* legal in Columbia!'

'Bestiality isn't,' mused Florence, between sips.

'Really?' asked Giles. 'I thought it was! Hold on. Let me check that.' He placed his cup and saucer back down on the patio table and pulled out his iPhone to do a quick Google search.

As Florence and Claire waited to see what he came up with, they quietly passed the joint to each other, neither feeling it necessary to make conversation.

After a couple of minutes, Giles exclaimed, 'Yes, it is! I've found their main tourist website, and there's a picture of some poor girl lying on a table, under a horse, with the title, "Things to do",' and he held out the phone for both Florence and Claire to see, who took it in turns to raise an eyebrow.

'Do you want some of this?' asked Florence, taking another pull on the joint as she looked over at Giles.

'Why not?' said Giles. 'It is tea time after all!'

As he took it from her, Margery re-emerged into the glorious summer's afternoon with what looked like a plate of chocolate brownies.

'Here you are. Fresh from the oven!' she said.

As they all enjoyed their tea, brownies and marijuana, Giles brought the conversation back to the proposed trade deal, asking, 'So, how much did the British Government want again?'

'I'm not sure,' answered Claire, 'but I'd have thought it would be quite a lot!'

'That sounds like a fair amount,' said Florence, looking over at Giles. 'Do we have that much?'

Giles, now gazing out over his vegetable patch, said, 'Huh?'

'Do you think we have enough to supply the whole of the UK?'

'It depends how much they want,' answered Giles, struggling to switch his attention back from watching his garden grow.

'I think they'd want quite a lot,' said Claire, again.

'That much?' said Giles.

'I'd have thought so,' said Claire.

'It does sound like a fair amount,' repeated Florence.

'What does?' asked Giles.

'How much they'd want!'

'And how much is that?'

'Quite a lot,' said Claire again.

'Would anyone like a chocolate brownie?' asked

Margery.

And as they all tucked in to the most delicious brownies that had ever been created by either man or womankind, Giles was able to emerge from his state of drug induced catatonia, enough at least to ask, 'How many people live in the UK, anyway?'

But nobody seemed to know.

After a few more minutes, during which time everyone's heightened sense of taste continued to explore the many complex flavours the brownies had to offer, Florence eventually asked, 'Does anyone know how many people live in the UK?'

This reminded Giles, who thought he'd better look it up on his iPhone before he forgot what they were talking about again.

Everyone else helped themselves to another chocolate brownie, and it wasn't long before he said, '64.1 million.'

Between mouthfuls, Florence asked, '64.1 million what?'

'People, living in the UK.'

'Oh!' she said. 'That sounds like quite a lot.'

Reaching for her third brownie, Claire thought she'd re-join the conversation. 'Sorry, how many did you say again?'

But Giles couldn't remember, so he looked back down at his iPhone before saying, '64.1 million,' once more.

As Claire tried to imagine what 64.1 million people looked like, and whether they'd all fit into a London bus, she asked Giles, 'Do you have that much?'

'That much what?'

'Marijuana?'

'Where?'

'Here.'

'On the table?'

'No, on the island?'

'Oh, probably not. But it wouldn't be difficult to expand production. We've got plenty of seeds, so we'd simply have to dig up all our potatoes and start growing marijuana instead.'

'More tea, anyone?' asked Margery.

They all nodded, and as she poured it out for them, Giles asked, 'When do you think they'd need it by?'

'I'm not sure, but I'd have thought it would be fairly soon. My uncle seems to be very keen.'

'And have you thought about distribution?' asked Giles, feeling increasingly lucid.

'A little. Once it's been legalised I think somewhere like Safebusy's would be interested.'

'And what about advertising?'

'Do you think we'd need it?'

'Well, it wouldn't do any harm.'

'No, I suppose not. I could probably meet up with an ad agency when I get back.'

'It may be a good idea to meet with Safebusy's first,' proposed Giles. 'There's not much point in advertising it until you have the distribution in place.'

'Makes sense,' said Claire. 'I'll see if I can arrange a meeting with them tomorrow.'

'When do you have to get back?' asked Florence, as she finished off her fourth brownie. 'It's just that Comrade Jeffrey is having a party on his yacht in Cowes tonight. Always great fun, and it would give you a chance to meet a few more of us Isle-of-Wighteans.'

'Well, I'd love to, but I haven't arranged for anywhere to stay.'

'Oh, don't worry about that! You'll be able to crash on the yacht. It's big enough! And I'm sure that Jeffrey would be more than happy to sail you across to England in the morning.'

Instantly falling in love with the idea of being able to wake up on board a massive yacht, and to enjoy breakfast whilst being sailed across the Solent, Claire agreed. She was supposed to come back that day, but she doubted that her uncle would mind, and even if he did, she'd simply tell him that it was all part of building future relations with the country who could well become their very first international independent trading partner outside of the European Union.

Chapter Fifteen
Buy more for less

Tuesday, 28th July
08:24 BST

EXTRAORDINARILY EARLY the next morning, Inspector Capstan was driving as fast as he could be bothered to, all the way from his home on the outskirts of Portsmouth down to Charlotte Street in the city's main shopping centre. His mobile phone had managed to beat his alarm clock to it that day, and by a good hour, thanks to Chupples, who'd taken great pleasure in calling him the moment he himself had been told about two cases of grand larceny that had taken place during the night; the first being at the big Safebusy's in town, and the second the local YouGet. As they'd both been closed at the time, and as they'd had their alarms disabled, the managers had only found out when they'd arrived to start their own day.

Arriving outside Safebusy's, he wasn't surprised to see Dewbush's car already there. The boy always drove around the place like an absolute lunatic, and as soon as he'd put the phone down to Chupples, Capstan had phoned Dewbush to order him to get straight down there to start taking statements. The main reason he'd done that was because he'd known that it would take him a while to get there himself. After all, he had to get out of bed, have a shave and a shower, enjoy a full English breakfast with some toast and a freshly filtered cup of coffee, get dressed, say goodbye to his wife and two children, open the front door, hobble down the path, climb into his car, start the engine, put the seatbelt on, adjust the position of the seat, as his wife must have used the car at some point, correct the angle of the rear-view mirror, for the same reason, re-tune the radio back to Radio One – the wife again – and drive off, all the while having to cope with his dodgy leg.

'Morning, Sir!' said Dewbush, appearing as if from nowhere to open the car door for him.

As Capstan placed his walking stick on the pavement and then used that, with the handle above the driver's door, to heave himself out, he said, 'For Christ's sake, Dewbush. You're still in your pyjamas!'

'Yes, I know, Sir.'

Straightening himself with a painful grimace, Capstan asked, 'And may I be so bold as to explore the reason why?'

'You told me to come down straight away, Sir, and I was still in bed at the time.'

'But I didn't mean for you to come to work in your pyjamas! This isn't some sort of fancy dress party where everyone's supposed to come as Arthur bloody Dent.'

'Arthur who, Sir?'

'Arthur Dent. You know, from the book, *The Hitch-Hiker's Guide to the Galaxy*?'

'I'm not with you, Sir.'

'No, and I'm most definitely *not* with you, not dressed up like that at any rate!'

'Shall I go home and get changed, Sir?'

Through gritted teeth, Capstan said, 'No! We'll finish up here first. But whatever you do, *DON'T* go back to the station before you change into something more suitable. Chupples would have me crucified if he'd known I'd let you walk around looking like - like that!'

'Oh, I'm sure he wouldn't go that far, Sir. Crucifixion is a very outdated form of punishment.'

'Shut up, Dewbush!'

'Yes, Sir. Sorry, Sir.'

'Right, anyway, what have you found out so far?'

'Well, Sir,' began Dewbush, who'd fortunately remembered to pick up his trusty notebook on the way out of the house, and pulling it out from one of his pyjama pockets, said, 'I left home at exactly 6:59, Sir, which meant that I was able to get here for just before seven thirty. I proceeded to Safebusy's main entrance, but the automatic doors didn't seem to be working. That's when I noticed the sign that said it didn't open until half past eight, so I've been waiting outside ever since.'

'So, basically, you've done absolutely nothing for the last hour?'

'Not exactly, Sir.'

'What *have* you been doing then?'

'I've been queuing up!' said Dewbush, in a defensive tone.

'But there's nobody else here!'

'Exactly, Sir! Which makes me first in line.'

But Capstan had had more than enough of his intellectually malfunctioning, moronically inept subordinate, and did what he should have done a very long time ago, and looked him straight in the eye and said, 'Dewbush?'

'Yes, Sir?'

'You're fired!'

'Really, Sir?' asked Dewbush.

'Yes, really! Now, sod off and leave me alone.'

'What, now, Sir?'

'Yes, please, and before I change my mind and have you demoted down to Sleeping Policeman, so that everyone in the UK can take it in turns to run you over without having to feel guilty about it.'

With Dewbush successfully dismissed, once and for all, Capstan turned to walk up towards the supermarket's main entrance. As he approached, the doors still didn't open automatically, so he looked down at his watch to check the time. That was when he noticed his Sergeant had followed, and was now standing directly behind him.

Turning back around, he said, 'I thought I told you that you were fired?'

'I assumed you were joking, Sir.' Dewbush gave him his normal happy-go-lucky sort of look. Before Capstan had a chance to fire him again, the supermarket's doors opened, and out popped a small middle aged man carrying a hefty sign.

'Oh, hello!' he said, a little out of breath. 'You're very early!' He placed the sign down and positioned it so that everyone coming in would clearly be able to see the message, EVERYTHING MUST GO! that had been spelled out in large, bold red letters.

'We're from Solent Police,' said Capstan, pulling out his formal identification. 'I'm Inspector Capstan and this,' he said, glancing back over his shoulder at Dewbush, 'I've got no idea who this is.'

Giving the person standing behind Capstan a peculiar look, the man said, 'You'd better come in then,' and led Capstan inside, leaving Dewbush to follow on after.

Looking up and around at the myriad of self-service counters and shopping aisles, along with numerous signs, posters and banners, all of which seemed to be advertising the same fact, that EVERYTHING MUST GO! Capstan asked, 'Are you the Store Manager?'

'Oh, sorry. I forgot to introduce myself. Yes, I am. My name's Derick Turpin. Forgive me, but it's always a little unsettling when a store gets robbed like this.' He gestured to various shopping aisles as if to prove that the place had, indeed been cleaned out.

Capstan looked at which aisles he seemed to be referring to, but couldn't see anything that was obviously missing, so he asked, 'And what did they take?' He deliberately omitted to add the word "exactly" at the end, as he had no intention of spending half an hour writing down what would only have been an extremely long and tediously boring shopping list.

'Oh, the normal really,' said the Store Manager, as if it happened every day.

'I see,' said Capstan, who wasn't aware that the store had ever been robbed before, not since he'd started working for the Solent Police at any rate. 'Does it happen often, then?'

'Not here, no. But I used to be the Store Manager for the Haringey branch in London. That was robbed on a fairly regular basis.'

'More than most, would you say, or was it in line with your other stores?'

'I must admit that we always seemed to be targeted more than the others, even those in London.'

'And may I ask who's been responsible for organising your marketing?'

'Ultimately I am, I suppose.'

'And did you use the same advertising in Haringey as you've done here?'

'Well, yes. But I really don't see the relevance.'

'It's just that it's occurred to me,' continued Capstan, 'and long before now I may add, that if you are going to advertise the fact that everything must go, then you shouldn't be too surprised to turn up one morning to find that everything has, indeed, gone.'

'Of course, but through the tills, and after having been paid for. Not in the middle of the night, when the place is locked up!'

'But it's not very clear though, is it?' Capstan continued. 'The signs all just say that everything must go. They don't detail the manner in which people should take it, or when they should do so.'

The Store Manager was now looking up at one of the larger banners that had been hung above the Fruit and Veg section, near to where they were standing; and with a furrowed brow, he said, 'You know what, Inspector, er..?'

'Inspector Capstan.'

'Inspector Capstan, yes, of course. You know you may have a point there. I'd never thought of it like that before.'

Noticing Dewbush still standing behind him, Capstan said, 'You'd better give my Sergeant here a list of what was taken, and then we can keep an eye out, just in case someone's stupid enough to start selling it down the local market.'

'Oh, right. Yes, of course. Well, it was mainly items from our frozen food section. Pepperoni pizzas, Cornettos, Viennartars, that sort of thing. They completely cleared out the freezers, and took everything from storage as well.'

'Have you made a note of that, Dewbush?' asked Capstan, thinking that he may as well use his Sergeant if he did insist on hanging around, despite the fact that he'd been fired.

'Yes, Sir,' said Dewbush, and read back from his notes, 'pepperoni pizzas, Cornettos, Viennartars, Sir.'

'Good! Right then. We'd better be off. But I suggest you take all that advertising down as soon as you can, and replace it with something a little less… ambiguous.'

'Quite right, Inspector. Quite right! And thank you for your help.'

'No problem. C'mon Sergeant. Let's drop into YouGet and see what's been going on there.'

Chapter Sixteen
The police sergeant in the striped pyjamas

08:47 BST

'ARE WE TAKING the car, Sir?'
'Yes, of course we're taking the car!'

'But the local YouGet is only just over there, Sir.'

'I know exactly where YouGet is, thank you very much, Dewbush, but I'm buggered if I'm spending any more time than is absolutely necessary standing anywhere near you, especially as the place is already filling up with shoppers. Actually, no! I've changed my mind. You can take your own car, and I'll take mine.'

'Right you are, Sir.' Capstan and Dewbush climbed into their respective cars and drove the fifty yards to the YouGet store before stopping to park, illegally, on the kerb.

'Hello, Sir!' said Dewbush, who'd managed to beat Capstan there by a good two minutes and was subsequently able to open the door for him.

'Are you still here, Dewbush?'

'Yes, still here, Sir!'

As Capstan started to heave himself out of his car for the second time already that day, he asked, 'So, you haven't hitched a ride on a passing spaceship, leaving

128

me and the rest of humanity to lay down our lives for the noble cause of building a brand new Intergalactic highway?'

Dewbush didn't have a clue what he was going on about, so he just said, 'You're such a kidder, Sir.'

'Yes, thank you, Dewbush. You must buy my stand-up comedy box set when it comes out at Christmas.'

'Oh! I didn't know you did stand-up, Sir!' As they approached the already open doors of the YouGet, he pulled out his notebook and pen from his pyjama pocket and asked, 'What's it going to be called?'

'What? My stand-up comedy box set?'

'Yes, Sir. If you tell me, then I can ask my Mum to buy it for me for Christmas.'

Capstan stopped, thought about it for a moment, and said, 'I think I'm going to call it *A Man called Doug*.'

Dewbush came to a halt beside Capstan so that he could write it down. 'It certainly sounds like fun, Sir. Is it any good? I mean, is it going to be funny?'

'Well, I haven't finished making it yet, but I suspect it will be - some of it at least. But I'm fairly sure the best bit will be when I invite a certain member of the audience to come up on stage to help me do my *What do you call a man with a shovel stuck in his head?* joke.

'Is that a good one, Sir?'

'A good joke? No, not really. But it will be when I take a sharpened shovel and hit him with it in such a way that it does stick out of his head.'

Capstan then turned to give Dewbush an unnerving sort of a look. 'Maybe you could help me with that bit, Dewbush?'

'Could I, Sir?'

'Why not, Dewbush? Why not indeed!' said Capstan, with a whimsical smile. 'Anyway, we're here now. Why don't you wait outside and let me go in on my own?'

'But what should I do out here, without you, Sir?'

'Surely you'll be able to find some sort of a queue to stand in?'

'I can't see one, Sir, and I'd rather come in with you. Everyone seems to be staring at me out here.'

'Really, Dewbush? How strange! Anyway, I suspect they'll stare at you just as much in there. Why don't you wait in the car?'

With that, Capstan turned to walk into the shop that was already filling up with customers, all seemingly desperate to spend their morning leafing through YouGet's five thousand page laminated catalogue in a bid to see if they could find something that they didn't already have two of.

'Hello, Inspector Capstan,' said a young man standing just inside the doors, who looked like he'd only just finished his GCSE's.

'Hello, Oliver,' said Capstan. 'I understand you've been robbed again?'

'I'm afraid so, but it's not AUT this time though,' replied Oliver, the store's manager.

'AUT?' asked Capstan.

'Oh, sorry. Appliance Upgrade Theft. It's what we've now termed the *on-going* problem.'

'The one when a customer buys a hand-held blender, or something, and then uses it in a threatening manner to upgrade to something more valuable?'

'And bigger. Yes, *that* one.'

'So what's happened this time?' asked Capstan, who was all too familiar with YouGet's AUT issue, and which was why they both knew each other by name.

'We've been fleeced, good n' proper, I'm afraid. They got in through the back and cleaned out half our stock!'

Capstan had a quick look around to see if he could spot any sort of misleading advertising, but couldn't, so he asked, 'Could you show me where they broke in?'

'Yes, of course.' He was about to lead the way when his eye was caught by a man standing directly behind Capstan who appeared to be wearing a pair of striped pyjamas. Somehow Dewbush had managed to take up his regular position without his boss seeing him.

'Is *he* with you?' asked Oliver.

Capstan nearly jumped out of his skin.

'For Christ sake, Dewbush! I was under the distinct impression that I told you to wait in the car!'

'I know, Sir. But I thought you might need me.'

'Really? I can't for the life of me imagine why.'

'It's Sergeant Dewbush, isn't it?' asked Oliver, the Store Manager.

'That's right! Sergeant Simon Peter Dewbush.'

'I'm sorry, Sergeant, er, Simon, Peter, Dewbush, but I didn't recognise you dressed up in that...costume.'

'Oh, it's not a costume. They're my pyjamas.'

'I see! Are you working undercover, or something?'

'I don't think so,' replied Dewbush. 'We're not working undercover, are we, Sir?'

'No,' said Capstan, 'but if we were, you'd blend right in.'

'Really, Sir?'

'Actually no, Dewbush. In fact it's probably more likely that you'd stick out like a man who'd just cut off his own thumb with a hacksaw, and was now walking around town asking if anyone's got a plaster.'

There was a moment's pause before Dewbush asked, 'Is that one of your jokes from your stand-up comedy box set, Sir?'

'That's right. It's from disc five.'

Oliver gave Capstan and Dewbush each a quizzical look, but as they seemed to have finished their rather strange conversation, he said, 'Well, anyway, you'd both better come through, I suppose, and I'll show you where they broke in.'

Leading them towards a small door to the left-hand side of the main customer pick-up desk, Oliver leaned over to carefully punch a number into the security key-coded lock. He pulled the door open and, standing to one side, gestured for Capstan and Dewbush to go through.

Capstan had never been into the rear Staff Only area before, and as his eyes adjusted to the low light level, he realised that he was in a vast, cavernous space that looked a little like an aircraft hangar but without any aircraft. It wasn't; it was just a warehouse lined with row after row of metal storage shelves that reached up to the roof, most of which were stacked to the brim with various shaped cardboard boxes. But it was still a fair size, when compared to the relatively small customer shopping area at the front.

'If you follow me,' said Oliver, his voice ringing through the cool dark air, and they followed his echoing footsteps.

Reaching a wall-sized corrugated iron door, Oliver said, 'This was open when I arrived,' and bending down, he took hold of a handle and heaved the whole thing up. As Capstan and Dewbush watched it rattle its way towards the roof, Oliver went on, 'Our loading bay is out here, where we normally keep our delivery trucks, but as you can see, they've also been stolen.'

'What did they take from inside?' asked Capstan.

'Mainly items from our weapons and munitions stores, but they did also take two boxes of sun lotion, a number of beach towels, about twenty deck chairs, badminton rackets, a cricket bat, a large patio table, six chairs and the table's umbrella. Oh, sorry, I nearly forgot. They also made off with a deluxe family-sized barbeque, along with three 13kg Propane gas bottles.'

Capstan glanced over at Dewbush, who thankfully was busy taking notes, before turning back to ask, 'You mentioned weapons and munitions. I assume you mean *plastic* weapons and munitions, for children?'

'Not exactly. All our shops keep a fairly extensive range of military grade weaponry.'

'I see,' said Capstan. 'But isn't that against the law?'

'Not at all,' replied Oliver. 'It's only illegal for members of the public to buy it. There's no law against it being sold.'

Now that Oliver had mentioned it, this strange nuance of the British legal system did ring a vague bell. However, it brought to mind another question.

'But if people can't buy it,' asked Capstan, 'then

what's the point of keeping it here to sell?'

'It's not for people, it's for the British Army. We have a contract with them, so they can buy as much as they like.'

'Oh!' said Capstan. 'Fair enough. And which particular weapons did they take?'

'All of them!'

'That sounds like a lot. You'd better run through the entire list. I have a feeling our Chief Inspector is going to want a full itinerary.'

'I may as well just give you the catalogue then,' said Oliver, as he made his way over to a torn cardboard box just inside the loading bay entrance. 'And I suppose I should mention that they took a box of these as well,' he said, handing one each to Capstan and Dewbush.

Looking down, the catalogue looked remarkably like the normal YouGet one, in that it was thick, heavy and fully laminated. But instead of having an orange and blue cover, it had a green and black one, and was called "YouGet Arsenal", instead of just "YouGet".

'Right then!' said Capstan. 'We'd better get back to the station. Thank you for your time, Oliver, but if you do intend to keep selling such potentially lethal items, it may be worthwhile bolstering up your security.'

'Unfortunately, Inspector, that's not a decision for me to make, but thankyou anyway, and I'll pass the idea on to Head Office.'

He gave Capstan a generous smile. 'You may as well go out the back here. If you just walk out through the loading bay area, you'll come out onto Brewer Street, which will lead you around to the front of the shop.'

With Dewbush making rapid notes of the directions, Capstan slipped out into the bright morning air, hoping to get back to his car before his pyjama-clad subordinate could catch him up.

Chapter Seventeen
The right place at the right time

12:09 BST

CLAIRE WAS FEELING more like a member of the Royal Family with every passing hour. The party on board Jeffrey's yacht had been an absolute blast, and she'd thoroughly enjoyed being introduced to all the key members of the Peoples' Independent Republic of the Isle of Wight. Having greeted what must have been at least fifty Isle of Wighteans, she felt she could curtsy and shake people's hands with the best of them, even whilst carrying a glass of Champagne. By the end of the night she'd become so well practised, she'd decided to update the Skills section of her Linked-in profile with her newly acquired ability, the moment she got home.

But if the party was good, waking up on board Jeffrey's sixty-five foot CloudCatcher sailing yacht to be invited to partake in an early breakfast on the aft deck was a sublime experience she would never forget. From there she was able to watch three exceptionally good-looking blonde n'bronzed crew members cast off the warps, motor the yacht out of Cowes harbour, position it head to wind and heave up the most beautiful pristine white sails that seemed to pierce the azure blue sky above, using nothing more than their perfectly toned muscular physiques. And as a delicately refreshing cool south-westerly breeze helped tilt the vessel onto one side, one of the able young crew members, who looked just as willing as he was able, steered the yacht over onto a port tack to begin crossing the Solent.

As she enjoyed watching the yacht cut through the undulating water that sparkled all around her, as if a trillion diamonds had just been lost over the side of a passing container ship, she was able to touch base with her uncle. Robert arranged for her to be picked up by his private helicopter from *No Man's Fort Hotel*, the exclusive luxury resort situated on the rather odd circular historical defensive structure that sits like a miniature island, just off Portsmouth's Esplanade. But as it boasts not one, but two helipads, along with a sizable sea-docking area, it made the perfect pick up point.

From there, Clare was flown to Vanguard Helipad on the Isle of Dogs in London's Docklands, where she was met by Robert's chauffeur and driven in style to a hastily arranged meeting with Safebusy's Chairman, Sir John Safebusy himself, at their head office on Farringdon Street, near Chancery Lane.

'Thank you for agreeing to meet at such short notice,' she said, as she was ushered into Sir John's lavish executive suite.

'It's my absolute pleasure,' he said, stepping from behind his opulent mahogany desk. And it *was* his absolute pleasure. Rarely did he have the chance to meet such a stunningly attractive young lady, not to discuss business at any rate, well, not *retail* business, and certainly not one who appeared to be wearing a completely transparent dress.

'It's not often that I'm asked by the Prime Minister himself to meet with one of his family members, and certainly never one who is so... delectable!'

He'd been emailed a picture of her, so going to some lengths to re-arrange his afternoon's schedule had been a no-brainer.

Claire blushed slightly, but with her now well-practised curtsy, she shook his hand and said, 'That is most kind of you.'

'May I introduce you to our Head of Marketing, Mr. Carl Lantern.'

Mr Lantern, who'd already stood up from the office chair in front of Sir John's desk, smiled at Claire and held out his hand.

Taking it, Claire curtsied again and said, 'How do you do?'

'No, how do *you* do?' he asked, with the usual intense level of personal interest most men had when meeting her for the first time.

'Do take a seat, won't you?' said Sir John, offering her the chair next to Carl's.

Once she'd sat down, Carl also made himself comfortable.

Sir John walked back around his desk to take his own seat. 'So, I've been hearing rumours that our Government is actually considering the idea of legalising cannabis. Is that true?'

'Well,' answered Claire, 'I've been advised that it's not so much a case that they're considering it, but more that they're going ahead, and simply need to pass it through Parliament and the House of Lords.'

'And may I ask what has brought about this rather sudden change of opinion on what has been a highly contentious subject since, well, since before I can remember?'

'My uncle thinks it will be good for his popularity.'

'No doubt it will, but that's hardly a good enough reason to legalise the national consumption of a substance that the rest of the modern world seems to have deemed as unhealthy, immoral, wholly inappropriate and, well, just categorically unacceptable, now is it?'

'Probably not, but you know Robert,' she said, and let out a nervous laugh.

'Yes,' said Sir John, 'I do, and all too well, I'm afraid.'

Safebusy's Head of Marketing cleared his throat.

'You have something you'd like to say, Carl?'

'If I may, Sir John.'

'Well, what is it, then?'

Shifting in his chair, Carl opened up the cover of his iPad and said, 'I took the opportunity before the meeting, Sir John, to do a little background market research into the, er, cannabis question, and with particular regard to its usage and popularity.'

Carl paused momentarily, keen for further confirmation that it was all right for him to continue.

'Yes? And?'

Feeling that was confirmation enough, Carl looked back down at his iPad and pushed on.

'In 2013 an estimated 232 million people had used the drug at some point in their lives, which is 4.9% of the global population. There isn't a huge amount of data available for the UK, but over in America it is estimated that in 2015, 43% of them had tried it. This is expected to increase by a staggering 8% this year alone; up to 51%! But what is most interesting is that around 12% of Americans are thought to have used it in the past year, with 7.3% having done so in the last month. Subsequently, it's generally considered to be the most commonly used illegal drug in the World.'

Carl paused again to gauge how all this was going down with Safebusy's Chairman. Sir John just kept staring at him, eventually saying, 'Go on! Go on!' which made Carl think that he'd better.

'So, if the British Government is going to legalise it, which it looks very much like they will, it's possible that it could become one of our best selling products. It could even outsell our frozen pepperoni pizzas! And from what I understand, one of the drug's side effects is to have an insatiable desire to consume a large amount of food, especially of the cake and biscuit variety. Apparently it is known as *having the munchies*. If that is the case, then it would naturally lead to an increase in sales of our Own Brand Sweet Baked range.'

Carl was clearly becoming excited by the prospect of being able to sell marijuana throughout every store in the UK, and now sat forward in his chair as he became increasingly animated.

'Furthermore, if we were able to agree some sort of exclusive distribution deal, then not only would we be able to out-perform our closest rivals, but it could be that we'd be in a position to mount a series of hostile takeover bids within just a few months of product launch, so gaining total monopolisation of the British marketplace. And given the fact that we're being forced to leave the EU, it may also help protect us against the forthcoming economic downturn, and go a long way towards bolstering up the British economy, ensuring that our customers continue to have sufficient liquidity to keep shopping with us, and not switch over to *One Pound & Ten Pence Land*, like they did during the last recession.'

Sir John leant back in his black executive's arm chair and let his Head of Marketing's passionate little speech permeate to the darkest recesses of his razor sharp, business-minded intellect. After a few minutes' silence, during which time neither Carl nor Claire dared say anything, he leaned forward, smiled at them both and said, 'I must admit that I wasn't wholly convinced by the idea when it was first mentioned to me, but it does sound like it has... potential. But we need to look into where we'd be able to source it from, and then come up with a suitable advertising campaign. And it wouldn't be enough to simply promote a half price special offer. We'd have to convince our core customer base that it's the sort of thing they could expect to find when wandering down the organic vegetable isle, without them all having a cardiac arrest. If we can't do that, then we may never see them again!'

'May I propose that I arrange to have an exploratory meeting with the advertising agency BOGOF, Sir John? From my experience, I'd have to say that they'd be the most likely to come up with something suitable.'

'Sounds sensible. But any thoughts about who we could buy it from?'

It was Claire's turn to take centre stage, and crossing her soft, elegant, lightly-tanned legs, she said, 'I may have a supplier for your consideration.'

Safebusy's Chairman and its Head of Marketing turned to stare at her.

'Really?' asked Sir John, with some incredulity.

'I spent the day yesterday on a formal visit to the newly established Peoples' Independent Republic of the Isle of Wight.'

'Oh, yes, I'd heard they'd had a referendum. Go on.'

'Well, as it happens, they've been farming marijuana for a number of years now, something they'd managed to keep quiet about since the Seventies. But since becoming independent, they're looking to expand production with the hopeful expectation of it becoming their main cash crop for export. If you were to approach them with some sort of exclusive partnership deal, before anyone else has a chance to, I suspect they'd be more than willing to come to a mutually beneficial agreement.'

'Right!' said Sir John. 'It would seem that we find ourselves in the right place at the right time, and in my experience that's a rare thing indeed! Carl, if you could arrange a meeting with BOGOF as soon as possible, and Claire, if you could give your contact on the Isle of Wight a call, then I think we may be in business.'

'Do you think it would be all right if Claire came with me, Sir John? She's clearly a key player in this, and

I could really do with her input.'

'I think that's up to Claire, isn't it?'

Adjusting his tie, Carl looked over at her.

'Would you like to come to see BOGOF with me? They're a highly regarded creative advertising agency, just down the road from here. It wouldn't be a date or anything, just a boring business meeting. But it would be great if you could come along.'

'That's sweet of you Carl. Thank you, and yes, I'd love to!'

Sir John looked at them both with parental pride, marred only by acute seething jealousy. He'd have given almost anything to have been the one to have gone out on a date with Claire, but he'd only just married his fourth wife, and if that one didn't work out, he'd be lucky if he could afford a retirement beach hut in Bournemouth.

'Good, that's settled then,' he said, making a concerted effort to remind himself of his all too recent marriage vows.

'Carl, take Claire, and let me know what they come up with. And Claire, if you can get the Peoples' Independent Republic of the Isle of Wight on board, I'll make sure you're compensated for your efforts. I may even be able to offer you a senior role here, if that would be of interest to you?'

'I'd be honoured to be considered, Sir John, thank you!' she said, thinking that if nothing else, another job offer would give her full justification for asking her uncle for an additional pay rise.

Chapter Eighteen
Mutual agreement

15:33 BST

'*CAPSTAAAAN!!!*'

'Did you hear something, Sir?'

But Capstan hadn't heard anything, as he'd only just shoved an entire Dark Chocolate Hobnob into his mouth. After taking several moments to masticate the biscuit enough to speak, he asked, 'Like what?'

Dewbush, who'd since driven home to change out of his pyjamas and into something more appropriate, answered, 'I don't know, Sir. But it sounded a bit like the Chief Inspector, calling your name, Sir.'

'Calling or shouting?'

'Probably shouting, Sir.'

'Well, I didn't hear anything, and anyway, if Chupples did want me, he'd just phone through on my direct line.'

As he reached for the coffee that he'd only just pulled out from the machine in the corridor, his desk phone started to ring, so he picked up the receiver instead and said, 'Capstan here!'

There was a momentary pause before he asked, 'What, now, Sir?' Then, 'Yes, Sir. Right away, Sir,' he said, and replaced the receiver into its cradle.

'C'mon Dewbush, His Majesticness wants a word.'

'The Chief Inspector, Sir?'

'Yes, Fun-Bag Chupples himself.'

'I wonder what he wants, Sir?'

'I've really no idea, Dewbush, but he's probably just read our reports on those two robberies.'

'That was quick, Sir. I mean, we only pushed them under his door five minutes ago.'

'I suspect it was more like ten, Dewbush, but even so, you're right. It was quick! He must have been in, after all.'

'We did listen outside his door, Sir. And it didn't sound like he was.'

'You're right again, Dewbush.'

'And another thing, Sir, I put a note in the suggestion box last week that said he should have something outside his door for everyone to leave their reports on, like a table. I thought it would save us having to disturb him all the time, Sir.'

Capstan stared over at his subordinate.

'That's a remarkably good idea, Dewbush. Well done!'

'Thank you, Sir. Maybe that's what he wants to talk to us about.'

'It's possible, but unlikely, I'm afraid. Anyway, he didn't sound very happy, so I suppose we'd better go and see what he wants.'

'Do you think I could take my coffee with me, Sir?'

'I suggest we both do, Dewbush. It is our tea-break after all. Actually, grab those Hobnobs! We may as well take them with us, too.'

'Yes, Sir.' Dewbush picked them up from the centre of the two grey Formica-topped desks that had been pushed together many years before, and from where he and Capstan had spent many a pleasant afternoon solving Solent's crime.

'They're nice, aren't they, Sir?'

'What, Dark Chocolate Hobnobs?'

'Yes, Sir. They're my favourites, Sir.'

'Mine too, Dewbush. In fact, I'd go so far as to say that life wouldn't be worth living without them. And they also perfectly complement a nice hot cup of coffee.'

'I completely agree with you, Sir.'

So, with two cups of instant coffee and a packet of Dark Chocolate Hobnobs, a rare, mutually-agreeing Capstan and Dewbush made the short trip down the corridor to heed the beck and call of their fastidious, disciplined, dedicated and hard-working Chief Inspector Chupples.

Chapter Nineteen
No biscuits

15:42 BST

HAVING KNOCKED on the door, Capstan poked his head in and asked, 'You wanted to see us, Sir?'

'Come in, will you please,' said Chief Inspector Chupples, who was sitting behind his desk, staring down at two pieces of white A4 paper. 'And do take a seat.'

As Dewbush closed the door behind them, Capstan said, 'Yes, Sir. Thank you, Sir,' and used his eyes, and the hand that wasn't holding his coffee, to instruct Dewbush to do the same.

After making themselves comfortable on the chairs immediately in front of their superior's desk, Dewbush leant forward and quietly asked, 'Would you like a Dark Chocolate Hobnob, Chief Inspector, Sir?'

Without allowing himself to be distracted by the highly inappropriate offer of a biscuit by the young Sergeant, and despite the fact that a furtive glance told him that they were his favourites, Chupples said, 'No, thank you, Bushdew!'

Taking one more look at the two pieces of paper on his otherwise empty desk, he turned them over, one at a time, to check that there was nothing on the back.

147

But there wasn't, so he looked up at Capstan and said, 'And these are your reports from last night's incidents, are they?'

'If you mean the two robberies in town,' said Capstan, craning his neck to see if he could recognise them. 'I believe they are, Sir. Yes.'

'I see,' said Chupples, looking back down at them again. 'I'd like to go through them with you, if that's OK?'

'Of course, Sir,' answered Capstan, as he began to extract a chocolate Hobnob from the packet that Dewbush was holding out for him. But it wasn't proving to be as easy as he'd expected it to be, as they'd all become stuck together due to either the heat of the day, or having been carried around by Dewbush.

'Have you quite finished?' asked Chupples, as he watched Capstan, who'd rested his walking stick against the desk in front of him, and his cup of instant coffee alongside that, and was now using both hands to try and unstick the top biscuit before wriggling it out from the packet.

'Nearly, Sir,' said Capstan, completing his task and taking a large bite.

Chupples shook his head. There was nothing for it. He was going to have to put up *yet another* sign outside his door to join the others, all of which were to deter his men from bringing what he felt were highly inappropriate items into his office. To date these signs included NO DOGS, NO ALCOHOL, NO HEADPHONES, NO SWEETS, NO RECREATIONAL BOOKS, NO MAGAZINES,

NO COMICS, NO PORNOGRAPHY, NO POKEMON CARDS, NO LEGO, NO AIRFIX MODELS, NO TOY TRAINS, NO SCALEXTRIC SETS, NO ACTION MEN, NO REMOTE CONTROLLED CARS OR HELICOPTERS, and the one that he thought had already covered the eating of biscuits, but clearly hadn't, NO FOOD. But he didn't mind too much. He enjoyed putting up signs, and they always seemed to have the desired effect. And so, making a mental effort to ignore the crumbs that were cascading down from the mouths of both Capstan and Dewbush onto his nice clean carpet, he pushed on.

'If we may first take a look at your report regarding the incident at Safebusy's supermarket, you say that, and I quote, "The shop was broken into at some point during the night, but as they only took some pizzas, ready meals and ice cream, it didn't seem like much of a big deal."

'That's the first paragraph,' said Chupples. 'The second, and what appears to be the final one, says, "Noticing that the Store Manager had put up lots of signs that said everything must go, we concluded that it was definitely his fault. So we told him to take them down and put up something else instead, like buy one, get one free, or something. The End."'

Capstan shot his Sergeant a menacing look. He'd asked Dewbush to write that report up whilst he ploughed on with the one for YouGet, but he'd forgotten to check it through before shoving it under Chupples' door.

'Apart from that being the worst report I've ever

read in my entire life, you do know that you're not supposed to finish them by writing, "The End" at the end, don't you, Capstan?'

'Yes, Sir. Of course, Sir.'

'I mean, we're not Hollywood script writers! We're policeman! Well, some of us are at any rate.'

'I know, Sir. Sorry, Sir. It won't happen again, Sir,' and without taking his eyes off Chupples, gave Dewbush's nearest leg a hearty kick.'

'Ow!' said Dewbush, staring at Capstan, who continued to fix his gaze on the Chief Inspector in front of him.

'Anyway,' said Chupples, who gave them both an odd look before continuing. 'The second one, which I can only assume is to cover the incident at the YouGet store, says, and again I may as well read directly from it, "At some point last night, thieves broke into the YouGet shop in town. They took a large number of items, most of which are included in the catalogue.'

Chupples looked up at Capstan and asked, 'And what catalogue is that?'

'They gave it to us before we left, Sir, but it wouldn't fit under your door, so we left it on the floor outside, in the corridor, Sir.' Before taking another bite from his biscuit, he said, 'Take a look to see if it's still there, will you Dewbush?'

'Yes, Sir,' replied Dewbush, who got up, walked over to Chupples' door, opened it and said, 'It's still here, Sir!'

'Could you bring it in?'

'Yes, Sir,' and he heaved it up with the hand that didn't still have the packet of Dark Chocolate

Hobnobs in it, and lumbered it back to Capstan.

'Here you are, Sir.'

'Well done, Dewbush,' said Capstan, who glanced down at it to make sure it was the right one, before handing it over to Chupples.

'It's their Arsenal one, I'm afraid, Sir.'

Unsure as to exactly what Capstan had meant by it being their "Arsenal one", but assuming it must have had something to do with football, Chupples laid it down on his desk so that it sat exactly perpendicular to the two pieces of paper, and began reading out loud again.

'"They also took three, or maybe four, delivery vans, which they must have used to transport the stolen merchandise."'

Chupples stopped once more.

'Didn't they know how many vans they'd had stolen?'

'They didn't seem to, no, Sir,' replied Capstan, unwilling to admit that he'd neglected to ask.

Chupples stared at Capstan for another moment, before continuing to read.

'"Concluding that the store had inadequate security to protect against the theft of the stolen items in question, it was advised that they *do something about it*."'

Having reached the end, or at least where the report stopped, Chupples looked up at Capstan and asked, 'But you haven't even said what was actually stolen!'

'Forgive me, Sir, but that was the bit when I mentioned about the vans and the catalogue, Sir.'

'So you're saying that all they took were catalogues and vans?'

'No, Sir. They took the *contents* of the catalogue, and the vans as well, Sir.'

'Oh, I see! Now I'm with you,' said Chupples, turning his attention to the catalogue in question. This was when he noticed that the cover featured a square-jawed, muscular man wearing a khaki-green sports vest, with a smouldering cigar hanging out of his mouth, and what appeared to be some sort of a bazooka in his hands.

'I thought this was their football catalogue?' Chupples asked, looking up at Capstan.

'How do you mean, Sir?'

'You said it was their Arsenal one.'

'That's right, Sir.'

'Oh, well I just thought that it would have had a more football themed front cover.'

As Chupples began to flick through its many hundreds of pages, Capstan thought he'd better clarify its theme.

'I think they're using the word in its original form, Sir, and not the name of a London-based football team.'

'You mean to tell me that — that — that they're selling what looks to be...advanced military weaponry?'

'I know, Sir. That's exactly what I said to them, but apparently they're allowed to, Sir.'

'How do you mean, they're allowed to? How can they possibly be allowed to - to sell—' and turning to the Hand Held Missile section, he read, 'FIM-92 Stinger Missiles, L2A1 ASM Anti-Structure Missiles, MBT LAW Anti-Tank Missiles and — and —and God knows what else?'

'Well, if you recall, Sir, the law states that members of the general public are not allowed to buy such items, but there's no legislation to prevent companies from selling them. And as it happens, YouGet has a contract with the British Army, Sir.'

Finally Chupples was able to put all the pieces of Capstan's rather vague report together.

'So, you're actually telling me that last night, YouGet was robbed, and that the thieves made off with the entire collection of weapons that were there as part of a sales contract with the British Army?' To emphasise the point, he flicked through all two thousand, four hundred and fifty-four pages of the very latest YouGet Arsenal catalogue.

'And the vans as well, Sir, yes.'

'And the vans as well?' repeated Chupples.

With his leg still smarting from the kick he'd received for no good reason, and in a subsequent effort to exact his revenge, Dewbush decided to try and make his immediate boss look like he hadn't been doing his job properly, and blurted out, 'They also took a large number of household garden items, Chief Inspector, Sir!'

Despite feeling Capstan's eyes burn into his skin, he pulled his notebook out and proceeded to read from the list he'd written down earlier that day.

'Two boxes of sun lotion, a number of beach towels, about twenty deck chairs, badminton rackets, a cricket bat, a large patio table, six chairs, the table's umbrella, a family-sized barbeque, and three 13kg Propane gas bottles.'

'Jesus Christ!' exclaimed Chupples, who'd begun to turn quite pale.

'I know, Sir,' said Dewbush. 'Inspector Capstan really should have included them in his report, Sir.'

Just before Capstan had a chance to drag Dewbush outside and beat the living shit out of him, Chupples' desk phone started to ring.

As Dewbush realised that he may have made a grave error in attempting to seek revenge for his sore leg, and one that could very well end up with him having broken arms, bruised ribs and a cracked skull to go with it, he asked, 'Shall I get that for you, Chief Inspector, Sir?'

'What?' asked Chupples, seemingly oblivious to the fact that his phone was still ringing. 'Oh, thank you, Bushdew, but no. I'd better get it,' and he picked up the receiver. 'Hello?'

There followed a brief pause before Chupples said, 'Okay, I'll tell them,' and put the phone down.

He turned his attention back to the catalogue and said, 'Morose wants to meet you,' before starting to flick through its all-too numerous pages again.

Nearly choking on the Hobnob that he'd only just wrenched out of the packet Dewbush was still tentatively holding on to, Capstan asked, 'Who, me, Sir?'

'Both of you, actually.'

Capstan fell into a stunned silence, leaving Dewbush, who'd begun to turn an off-white sort of colour, to ask, 'Did - did he say why, Chief Inspector, Sir?'

'I've no idea. Maybe he wants to throw you off the

top of the prison walls.'

'He c-c-can't do that, can he?' asked Dewbush, completely forgetting to add the required "Sir" at the end.

Such a blatant show of disrespect from such a low-ranking officer was enough to snap Chupples out of his former state of mild shock.

Slamming the catalogue closed, he said, 'Rarely have I met two such totally inept, mentally deficient policemen! I had a bad enough opinion of you both when I was a Detective Inspector, but now that I've seen first-hand what Morose must have had to put up with, frankly, I'm not surprised he went mad and started killing off half the town's residents. It's just a shame that he didn't add the pair of you to his list! If I have to put up with any more of - of…this,' he said, looking down at the reports and the YouGet Arsenal catalogue, 'I wouldn't be surprised if I did the same! So anyway, I really don't care what Morose wants with you, but one thing I do know; that if you don't get down there this minute, you're both fired. Did you hear me? *FIRED!* And I'll make sure that you don't even qualify for a pension! Now fuck off please, before I change my mind and have some highly incriminating evidence planted on you so that you can spend the rest of your lives behind bars, getting chummy with Morose and all his new friends.'

As neither Capstan nor Dewbush had ever heard Chupples to use the "f" word before, or even mention the traditional police practice of planting evidence in order to make an effective arrest, they decided that he must mean it. So they eased themselves out of their chairs, retrieved their respective coffees, Capstan's stick and the now half-empty packet of Hobnobs; and muttering, 'Yes, Chief Inspector, Sir,' in unison, they made a hasty retreat, closing the door as quietly as possible so as not to give him any more reason to get upset with them.

Chapter Twenty
How to get a cup of tea in advertising

16:03 BST

'HELLO, CARL, good to see you again,' said Ben Gothenburg, BOGOF's Creative Director, as he welcomed Claire Bridlestock and Carl Lantern into the plush boardroom office on one of the top floors of the famous Gherkin building in the City of London.

'Hello, Ben,' said Carl with a vigorous hand shake. 'How are you?'

'Very well, thank you! I believe you already know my colleagues, Jacob Hovel and Stan Thornton.'

Carl shook hands with Jacob and Stan. 'I'd like to introduce you to Claire Bridlestock,' he said, and stepped to one side to give them all a clear, unobstructed view.

'How do you do?' she said to them all, adding her little regal curtsy. But the way in which the late afternoon sun was streaming in through the large office windows, all three of BOGOF's employees could see straight through her dress, leaving them wholly captivated by her hedonistic beauty. So they just stood there, opened mouthed, completely forgetting to either offer a hand to shake or even to say hello.

Sensing the potential awkwardness of the situation, Carl thought he'd better elaborate on his initial introduction.

'Claire is the Prime Minister's Marketing and PR Consultant, and also just happens to be his niece, and a key player in what we'd like to talk to you about, so we thought it made good sense to invite her along.'

'Y-y-yes, of course,' stuttered Ben, and the three advertising executives all began offering her their chairs at the same time.

Choosing the closest, which happened to be Stan's, she gave him a pleasant smile, said, 'Thank you very much,' and sat down and made herself comfortable, crossing her smooth naked legs.

Carl was offered the seat next to Claire, and they all took it in turns to choose a chair around a circular boardroom table designed to exactly resemble an enormous jar of Marmite, but one that had been flattened out in such a way that it may have been stepped on by a giant, or a dinosaur, or a giant riding on the back of a dinosaur as they searched for something to put on a piece of toast that they'd both be able to enjoy.

'Can I offer you a tea, or maybe a coffee?' asked Ben.

'A cup of tea would be nice,' said Carl.

'Tea for me as well, please,' said Claire, who probably didn't need another one, but felt obliged to accept the offer.

'Stan, will you do the honours, please.'

Stan Thornton, BOGOF's Junior Client Account Manager, who'd been doing his absolute best *not* to stare directly at Claire's ample young breasts, both of which he could see as clearly as if she'd turned up topless, welcomed the distraction.

'Yes, of course!' he blurted out, but having only just sat down, realised that the prospect of standing up again really didn't appeal, especially as his gentleman's area was already doing something very similar. So to delay the prospect of having to show everyone in the room just exactly how he felt about their new guest, he asked, 'Would you like milk and sugar, or maybe some milk but with no sugar? Or perhaps you'd like absolutely no milk but with just a tiny bit of sugar?'

'Milk and one sugar would be nice,' said Carl, tagging 'Thank you,' onto the end.

'I'll have the same,' said Claire, with another vivacious smile.

Stan still wasn't in the least bit ready to get up, and having been on the receiving end of what he considered to be a highly provocative facial gesture, was probably in a worse state. So he thought he'd narrow down their choice. 'Earl Grey, Darjeeling, English Breakfast or PG Tips?'

'Earl Grey for me,' answered Carl, and looked over his shoulder at Claire.

'Earl Grey for me as well,' she said.

'And would you like white sugar or brown?'

'Could I have white sugar please?' asked Carl.

'Same for me, thank you,' said Claire.

'Granulated or caster?'

'I'd prefer granulated, if you have some,' said Carl.

'Me too,' said Claire.

'And what sort of milk would you like?' asked Stan, pulling out a pen to take notes.

Carl was beginning to tire of this traditional English

ritual of being asked how he'd like his tea every time he met with a client. He'd never had to choose from a selection of milk before, though. 'May I enquire as to what sort you have?'

'We have powdered, condensed, evaporated, skimmed, semi-skimmed, and full fat.'

'Could I have the semi-skimmed one?' said Carl.

'And for me?' requested Claire.

'Organic?' asked Stan.

'If you do happen to have organic, then I think we'd both prefer it,' answered Carl, with a quick glance over at Claire for confirmation.

'And would you like Fair Trade?'

'Again, yes I think we would.'

'And Free Range?' asked Stan again, glancing up from his notes.

'Oh,' said Carl, 'I thought that was just for eggs?'

For the briefest of moments Stan glanced at Carl as if he'd just fallen off a passing Brazilian Banana Boat, but with the application of a generous smile was able to hide his look of contemptuous conceit. 'The term was originally used only for egg production, yes, but it's since been rolled out to encapsulate all produce being extracted from intensively farmed animal livestock.'

'So, a Free Range Cow is, what, one that is allowed to roam...free?' asked Carl, trying hard not to sound as if he was a bit behind the times.

'I suspect that it would be too dangerous to let them wander around wherever they liked, but I believe they are allowed to stand in a field.'

Keen to move the subject on from how they

wanted their tea to what they'd actually come to talk about, Carl said, 'Could we both have Free Range Milk please?'

'No problem at all,' said Stan. Having completely forgotten about Claire and his earlier state of physical arousal, he picked up his note pad, stood up and headed over to a bright orange cabinet in the corner of the boardroom that seemed to house a bounty of cups, jugs, jars, bowls, containers and baskets, each one overflowing with produce.

Seeing that the tea was now successfully in production, BOGOF's Creative Director, Ben Gothenburg, brought the subject around to what they'd all come to discuss, and looking over the table at Carl, said, 'You mentioned on the phone something that, well, to be perfectly honest, we're all rather excited about.'

'Great news, isn't it?' said Carl.

'And about time too!' agreed Ben.

'Yes, and Sir John's very much on board with the idea. We also have a supplier, thanks to Claire here, so we thought we'd pop over to see if you have any initial thoughts as to how best we could go about advertising it?'

Leaning back in his lime green leather executive's arm chair, Ben entwined his fingers together and gave sagacious contemplation to the ceiling above.

'It's a tricky one, isn't it?' he said.

Next to him, Jacob, BOGOF's Senior Client Account Manager, who'd decided to emulate his boss by also entwining his fingers and sitting back in his own leather executive's arm chair, his being more of an aqua blue colour, agreed. 'It certainly is!'

'It's just that it's been a banned substance for such a long time,' continued Ben, 'that I suspect it's going to take something really rather special to counteract the negative connotations that have surrounded the product since, well, probably since Woodstock!'

'I couldn't agree more,' added Jacob.

'Especially when Safebusy's core customer base isn't exactly open to trying new products, and certainly not formerly illegal ones!'

'They certainly aren't,' confirmed Jacob.

Returning from the corner of the room, Stan placed two bone china tea cups and saucers down in front of Claire and Carl. 'Two cups of Earl Grey tea, each with a teaspoon of white caster sugar and a splash of organic, fair trade, free range, semi-skimmed milk.'

Carl and Claire took it in turns to say, 'Thank you,' and they each lifted their respective cups to take a tentative sip of the contents, giving Stan time to return to his chair, which was either luminous yellow or lime green; it was difficult to tell.

'However,' said Ben again, 'we are extremely confident that we'll be able to come up with something for you,' and he leant forward to place both his elbows on the table, keeping his fingers firmly entwined.

Jacob followed suit, and backed up his boss by repeating, 'We're *extremely* confident!'

'That's great,' said Carl. 'So, do you have any ideas that you could perhaps come up with now, for me to take back to Sir John?'

'What, today?' asked Ben, with a startled look.

'Well, I'm sure he's not expecting a full creative pitch or anything, but just a couple of ideas, perhaps?'

'I see,' said Ben. 'But unfortunately it takes us weeks, if not months, to come up with creative concepts.'

'Yes, we appreciate that, but Sir John is keen to move quickly on this.'

'I mean, we don't just pluck them out of thin air. And we certainly wouldn't be comfortable to offer you something simply from off the top of our heads. You do understand, don't you?'

'Of course, but I think Sir John would still like it if we could take something back to him today, just so that he knows the sort of thing you'd have in mind.'

'Right,' said Ben, and leant back in his chair again to resume his former position of staring up at the ceiling.

As the room fell into what felt like an awkward silence, Carl glanced over at the two other BOGOF employees, but they were also leaning back in their chairs, with their fingers locked together, gazing up into space.

Hoping that they'd all become engaged in a complex process of creative consideration, and hadn't simply decided to ignore him, Carl thought he'd let them get on with it for a while and took another sip from his tea.

A minute or two later, Jacob leaned forward in his chair to start drawing something on the A4 notepad he had in front of him. And after a few moments he was able to announce, 'I think I may have something!'

'Are you sure?' asked Ben, looking at him over the bridge of his nose, but still leaning backwards, facing up towards the ceiling.

'I think so, yes!'

'You don't think you should run it by me first, in private?'

Jacob looked down at the sketch he'd made and said, 'I'm fairly confident about it.'

'Right! Well! You'd better go ahead then!'

'Okay.' With a degree of animated excitement he began to describe his idea.

'Imagine the scene of Safebusy's supermarket during a normal busy Saturday afternoon. Suddenly a group of armed gunman break in, all in brown removal men's overalls and wearing black ski masks, and they rush up to the cigarette and magazine counter and start shouting. "GIVE US THE WEED! GIVE US THE WEED!" or something like that. Anyway, without breaking a sweat, the girl behind the till simply pops a box of it into a bag and hands it to them with a wholesome smile and says, "That will be £4.50 please." That's when Safebusy's logo comes up and underneath it says, "Cannabis. Now legally available from your local Safebusy's."'

'That really is rather good!' said Ben, sitting forward again to make some notes of his own.

'Er,' said Carl. 'It is good, of course, but I don't suppose you could come up with something without the armed robbery bit.'

'Really?' said Ben. 'I thought that worked rather well.'

'I did like it, obviously,' Carl said, 'but just wondered if we could have an alternative idea, perhaps. Maybe something that would help to disassociate it from its former gangland connection?'

'I've got it!' cried Jacob, as he made a frantic sketch before grinning down at what he'd drawn.

Ben stared at him from what was probably considered to be the head of the table, expecting Jacob to tell them exactly what he thought he had; but realising that he was probably waiting for permission, said, 'Don't just keep it to yourself, Jacob. Come on, out with it!'

'Okay, well,' began Jacob, looking almost as if he was rather desperate to go to the loo.

'Imagine an old woman sitting in front of the TV, doing some knitting, or something, but instead of having a pot of tea beside her, she has a bowl of marijuana, along with an ashtray with a really large spliff in it. As she sparks it up to take her first toke, the police break down her door, storm in, pick her up and slam her face into the floor, or maybe the wall. And just before she's carted away she cries out, "I BOUGHT IT FROM SAFEBUSY'S! I BOUGHT IT FROM SAFEBUSY'S! THE RECEIPT'S IN MY HANDBAG!" Then one of the armed policemen could say, "She's right, Sarge. The receipt *is* in her handbag," and as the Sergeant leads his men out, the Safebusy's logo comes up again, with the same strapline. "Cannabis. Now legally available from your local Safebusy's."'

'Excellent, Jacob! Really good! I think that presents the perfect juxtaposition between legality and consumer confidence. Well done!'

Carl and Claire exchanged looks of mutual concern, leading Carl to say, 'Yes, that really is remarkably good, but perhaps we could have something a little less…violent? Maybe an idea that highlights the many benefits of smoking marijuana, as well as the fact that it's now available from Safebusy's?'

Ben folded his arms and stared over at Carl.

'As I said earlier, it will be tricky to come up with a single ad that meets all the brief's objectives, so it would probably be best to run a series of different ones, each using the same strapline that Jacob here's come up with, so that they follow a similar theme. Do you have any other ideas, Jacob?' he asked, looking over at his colleague.

'How about we have some guy being released from prison, and the very first thing he does is to pop into the nearest Safebusy's store, which could be directly opposite the prison's main gate. Then we could see him coming out a few minutes later, skinning up and taking a few tokes. And as a satisfied smile spreads over his face we could have the same strapline coming up.'

With his own smile of professional satisfaction, Ben Gothenburg finished the story off for him by saying, '"Cannabis. Now legally available from your local Safebusy's." I really like it, Jacob. I like it a lot!'

But neither Carl nor Claire looked particularly convinced, and raising her hand a little, Claire said, 'I'm not a creative advertising person, or anything, but couldn't we just have a housewife returning from having dropped off her children at school to start their first day back after the long summer holidays. She could head out onto her patio to enjoy a peaceful, relaxing smoke with the only thing to distract her being the mellow song of a blackbird in a nearby tree? And then the strapline-thing could say something like, "Unwind naturally with Safebusy's Fair Trade Marijuana"?'

The three BOGOF employees all stared at her, and Carl too, before Ben said, 'I must admit that I think all the suggested ideas have possibilities. What we now need to do is to sit down with our full creative team to come up with a concrete plan that we could present to Sir John.'

'I think that's very sensible,' said Carl, unable to shake the feeling that they'd have been better off just asking Claire to come up with the advertising campaign.

'Shall we call it a day?' he said, pushing back his chair.

This prompted everyone else in the room to do the same, and after they'd all managed to shake hands, Stan led Carl and Claire out of the boardroom and to the lift door that opened directly opposite their reception desk.

'It was certainly very nice to meet you,' said Stan, aiming the comment mainly at Claire, 'and if you need to discuss anything with me, at any time, day or night, or even in the evening, maybe on Friday, at eight o'clock, over a drink inside the Badger and Hamster on Brewer Street, near Piccadilly Circus, you can contact me on that number.'

Taking the business card that he was offering, Claire said, 'Thank you, Stan. I'll certainly keep that in mind,' and as the lift door pinged open, Carl and Claire stepped inside to start the long journey all the way down to the Gherkin's ground floor lobby.

Chapter Twenty One
Where there is light,
there shall be darkness

16:17 BST

HAVING PUSHED and shoved their way through what felt like half the country's press, but was probably only about one percent of it, as the rest were being kept busy covering all the other British prisons that were still under the control of their inmates, Capstan and Dewbush found themselves at the same gate that they'd stood in front of just the morning before.

'Push the intercom button, will you, Dewbush?'

'Do I have to, Sir?'

'Yes, of course you have to! And you'd better be quick about it, before that lot recognises us,' and Capstan glanced over at the press, who were fortunately all too busy training their cameras along the prison walls, hoping to see some more bodies being thrown off, to have noticed their arrival.

'Right you are, Sir,' said Dewbush, and leaned forward to give the grubby white plastic button a tentative push.

'*Who the fuck is it?*' came an almost instant metallic reply.

Jumping back with a start, Dewbush looked at Capstan and said, 'I don't suppose you'd like to do all the talking, would you, Sir?'

Since their interrogation inside a German military prison the year before, Dewbush had become a little more mindful of saying anything at all whenever confronted by a potentially hostile situation.

Leaning forward in his place, Capstan said, 'It's Detective Inspector Capstan and Sergeant Dewbush. We understand that, er, Morose would like to speak to us.'

Capstan stood up straight, hoping that they'd be able to conduct the meeting without having to go in, like last time. But unfortunately for both of them, the same voice came back saying, '*You'd better come in then, hadn't you?*' and a loud buzzer vibrated from the gate.

Unwilling to show fear in front of his Sergeant, and despite the fact that he really didn't want to, Capstan said, 'C'mon Dewbush. Let's go and see what the old bastard wants.'

'If you say so, Sir, but may I suggest you don't call him that. Not directly to his face, at least, Sir.'

Capstan pushed open the gate to begin walking towards the prison's main entrance. 'Don't worry Dewbush, I'm not that indelicate.'

'Perhaps it would be better if we kept calling him Chief Inspector, Sir?'

'In all honesty, I really don't think that would be appropriate, Dewbush.'

'Maybe he's started using a criminal name that we're supposed to refer to him as, Sir?'

'What, like the Psychotic Serial Slasher of

Southampton and the South Coast?'

'Yes! Like that one, Sir.'

'Well, I doubt it.'

'But he might have, Sir.'

'No, you're probably right. Tell you what, when we meet him, why don't you start the conversation off by saying, "Good afternoon, Mr Psychotic Serial Slasher of Southampton and the South Coast. How are you today?" I reckon that would set the perfect tone, don't you think?'

'It would if we both did, Sir.'

'You can if you like, but I think it would be a bit of a mouthful for me.'

As the ancient doors of Portsmouth Prison loomed ever larger, Dewbush began to rehearse his introduction, repeating, 'Good afternoon Mr Psychotic Serial Slasher of Southampton and the South Coast,' over and over again to himself. But after a while he gave up and said, 'I think you're right, Sir. There are too many words beginning with S, and I'm not even sure they're in the right order.'

At the prison's main entrance, the solid oak doors remained firmly closed, and as Capstan couldn't see anyone awaiting them, he looked around for something else to use to say that they'd arrived. Seeing an old black cast iron hand-pull, he gave it a tug, and heard a bell ring inside. He stood back a little as he heard a number of bolts being drawn. One of the doors was slowly pulled inwards, so creating a narrow gap that was just wide enough for him and his subordinate to squeeze through.

Stepping into the cool oppressive shadow beyond,

it took a few moments for Capstan's eyes to adjust from the stark contrast of the brightness of the day outside. But even before they'd done so, he could make out that the inmate who'd been sent down to meet them was laden with advanced military weaponry, the most obvious being an L85A1 assault rifle which he pointed first at Capstan and then at Dewbush, as if undecided as to which one to shoot first.

'Who's Detective Inspector Cat Sperm and who's Sergeant Bush Stew?' the gunman asked, as he continued to switch the dangerous end of the gun from one to the other.

'Oh, um, well,' said Capstan, who for once in his life wasn't keen either to correct the mispronunciation of his name, or to own up to the fact that he was, indeed, a Detective Inspector.

Dewbush came to his rescue. 'I'm Sergeant *Dewbush*, and this is Inspector *Capstan*. We're from the Police!'

There was a momentary pause as Capstan winced in preparation for being shot in the head. However, the heavily armed inmate simply said, 'Stay there,' and walked around behind them to slowly close the heavy 16th century door, so plunging them into what Capstan felt to be an all-consuming darkness. And as he stood there, eyes ever widening in the vague hope that he might actually be able to see something, he listened to three heavy cast iron bolts being slid back into place, one after the other.

Once the door had been secured, the gunman said, 'Follow me,' and Capstan heard him walk around to the right of him, and then off into the distance. But as

Capstan still couldn't see a thing, and subsequently had no idea where it was that the armed inmate was going, he thought it best to stay exactly where he was until someone had the foresight to turn a light on.

'Aren't you coming, Sir?' came Dewbush's voice from the blackness ahead.

'No, Dewbush. I'd thought I'd stay here for a while, just in case they decide to show a movie.'

'Er, I don't think they will, Sir.'

'They're bound to,' answered Capstan. 'And there'll probably be a girl along in a minute with a torch, selling popcorn.'

'And the man did tell us to follow him, Sir.'

'You're not seriously telling me that you can actually see anything, are you, Dewbush?'

'Of course, Sir. But I've always been good at seeing in the dark.'

'A bit like being hung upside down, I suppose?' enquired Capstan.

'That's right, Sir. But I'm fairly sure that I'm not a Vampire any more, Sir,' continued Dewbush, in his usual conversational tone. 'I asked my Mum about it, and she said that they don't exist. She reckons that the reason I'm good at being hung the wrong way up is because I went through a phase of eating bananas when I was young. According to her, the fact that I enjoy the odd glass of red wine and that I need to wear sun lotion on holiday is fairly normal. So, I think that I'm either most definitely *not* a Vampire, Sir, or that if I am one, then there are quite a few of us around.'

'So you're telling me that I don't need to rush out and buy a sharpened shovel so that I can cut your head off before burying you in a graveyard that's been blessed by the Sacred Holy Virgin Mary's godmother, then?'

'Yes. I mean, I don't think so, Sir. No.'

'Shame.'

'If you take hold of my hand, Sir, I can lead you out.'

'Are you honestly suggesting that we hold hands, Sergeant?'

'Only if you want to, Sir?'

'Of course I don't bloody want to!'

'You could place your hand on my shoulder?'

'Where's that?'

'It's right here, Sir.'

'Look, just give me your arm, and I'll hold on to that.'

From out of the darkness, Dewbush took hold of his boss's hand and rested it on his arm, to begin leading him through the blackness towards their impending meeting with Morose, the former Chief Inspector of the Solent Police, but now the Head of COCK, the largest and most formidable of Britain's many criminal organisations.

Chapter Twenty Two
What's in a name?

16:29 BST

'I'VE GOT TWO policeman to see you, Gov.'

'Show then in, please,' said Morose, sitting behind his new desk in his brand new office, with his two bodyguards, Bazzer and Gazzer, standing just behind and each to one side of him, as they weren't currently being paid to.

The office itself had until very recently belonged to Mr Oliver Obtuse, the late Prison Warden, whose body lay at the base of the main prison wall, along with all the rest of Portsmouth Prison's former employees. But it made a comfortable enough centre of operations for Morose, and was certainly more practical than the cell that his predecessor, Harry Humpty, had used.

'Yes, Gov,' said the inmate, but it was only then that he realised that they weren't behind him, as he thought they'd been, so he stared down the long dark corridor and shouted, 'OI, YOU'S TWO! ARE YOU COMING OR WHAT?'

An irritated voice came echoing back, saying, '*Give us a minute! We're not all nocturnal, you know!*'

'*I am!*' said another voice, with a slightly higher, cheerful tone to it.

Morose recognised both voices immediately and

shuddered.

'WELL, HURRY UP! WE AIN'T GOT ALL FUCK'N DAY!' shouted the inmate, before he turned back to Morose to say, 'Sorry Gov, they must have gotten lost on the way.'

'It's not your fault, Bill. Those two would get lost inside a telephone box.'

A couple of minutes later, Dewbush's head popped momentarily around the corner, saw Morose, smiled at him, and then retreated as he called back down the corridor, 'I think we've found it, Sir!'

Having already reached the office door, Capstan said, 'Yes, I can see that, thank you, Dewbush!'

'Inspector Capstan and Sergeant Dewbush,' said Morose, not bothering to get up. 'How good of you to come. And at such short notice as well!'

'Hello, Mr Morose, Sir,' said Dewbush, which was how he'd finally decided to address his former Chief Inspector, who'd since become a mass-murdering criminal mastermind.

Catching his breath, Capstan stood up straight, leaned on his stick and said, 'Hello, Morose. I see you've been keeping yourself busy.'

'Busy enough.'

'And how's prison life treating you?' Capstan asked, glancing up at the two giant men standing just behind and to each side of him.

'Remarkably well, thank you for asking,' said Morose, backing up his words with a wide grin. 'I hear that young Charlie Chupples is now your new Chief Inspector.'

Capstan hadn't known what Chupples' first name

was until then; but now that he did, it explained a lot.

'That's right,' he answered.

'And how's he getting on?'

'Well enough,' said Capstan, feeling unusually reticent to make any further comments, and keen to move the subject along. 'So, you wanted to see us, then?'

'That's right. I did!' said Morose. 'Take a seat, will you?' and he gestured to the two wooden chairs directly in front of his desk.

Capstan motioned Dewbush to sit down, and as they both made themselves comfortable, Morose continued, 'You may or may not be aware that, since the recent demise of the notorious Harry Humpty, God rest his soul, I've found myself to have been appointed the new Head of the Centre for Organised Crime and Kidnapping which, as I'm sure you're aware, is known throughout Europe and quite possibly the world as COCK, for short.'

Dewbush blurted out a laugh. He'd never heard of it before, and the sudden use of such a singular acronym had caught him off guard.

Morose and Capstan each shot him a look of contemptuous indifference.

'As I was saying…'

The news, however, made Dewbush think of a question, which he thought he'd take the opportunity to ask by raising his hand.

'Yes, Dewbush. You'd like to ask something?'

'Does that mean we should now refer to you as the Cock's Head, Sir?

'I'm sorry, Dewbush, I'm not with you?'

'I was just wondering if we should start calling you the Cock's Head, Sir, instead of Morose, or Mr. Morose, or Mr. Chief Inspector Morose, or Mr. Chief Inspector Morose of the Solent Constabulary, or Mr Morose, Chief Inspector of the Solent Constabulary who's since become the Psychotic Serial Slasher of Southampton and the South Coast, Sir?'

'I really don't mind what you call me, Dewbush.'

'It's just that I'm used to calling you Chief Inspector, Chief Inspector, Sir, but Inspector Capstan here says that it's not appropriate anymore. But I don't really know what else to call you, Sir. So I think, if I *could* call you the Cock's Head, then I think I'd like that.'

'As I said, Sergeant Dewbush, I'm not sure I care, all that much.'

'Or maybe we could simply shorten it to Cockhead, Sir? Or how about the Big Cockhead, Sir, being as you're so large, and everything. And now that you've shaved your head, and with that new beard thing that you've got going on, I'd have to say that the name would really suit you, Sir.'

As Capstan stared at his subordinate with unqualified disbelief, Morose answered, 'How about we just stick to Morose, Dewbush?'

'Right you are, Sir,' and he retrieved his trusty notebook and pen to make a note of it.

'Okay,' said Morose, with a deep, calming breath. 'Where were we?'

'We were just trying to decide what to call you,' said Dewbush, glancing up from his notes.

'Oh, yes. Well, now that that's settled, I'd like to

move on to what I wanted to talk to you about.'

'Do you mind if I take notes, Mr Morose, Sir? I've got my notebook out now, so I thought I may as well.'

Feeling increasingly like he was back at his old job again, Morose said, 'What a splendid idea, Dewbush. Well done!' with more than a hint of sarcasm.

'Thank you, Mr Morose, Sir,' replied Dewbush, before momentarily looking down, and then up again to ask, 'You were saying, Mr Morose, Sir?'

'Quite! As I was saying, Sergeant Dewbush. I was saying...er...?'

'You were saying, Mr Morose, Sir, that it was okay for me to take notes.'

'WILL YOU SHUT THE FUCK UP, DEWBUSH! FOR CHRIST SAKE!'

Dewbush decided it best if he did just that, and returned to his notes, but decided to omit that last comment.

Capstan, meanwhile, couldn't help but smile with wistful reminiscence. It really was just like the good old days.

'As I was saying,' re-started Morose, again, 'I *am* now the Head of COCK! I'm also in charge of Portsmouth Prison, along with all its inmates, and those up and down the country. Furthermore, as I've no doubt you've become acutely aware, we're heavily armed. And so, with all that in mind, I'd like to make a few...requests.'

'You mean demands?' asked Capstan.

'Actually, yes. That would be the more accurate word. Thank you, Capstan.'

'And may I ask what they are?'

'I'd like a plane to be allowed to land at Gatwick tomorrow evening, at around half-past nine.

'Right. And?'

'And I'd like its contents to pass through customs without being searched. And then I'd like some of my men to be allowed to load it up onto a few trucks and drive it back here, to me.'

'I see,' said Capstan. 'And if the powers that be decide that they don't wish to help you to import whatever it is that you wish to illegally bring in to the country, what will you do? I mean, it's not as if you have any hostages, or anything, now is it?'

'Ah yes, Capstan, I can see that you're still as bright as a shiny new button that's become stuck under the shoe of a wandering alcoholic. You're right, of course, we don't have any more hostages, but only because you failed in the relatively simple task of delivering a few ice-creams on time. So anyway, your inability to do…anything, really, forced me to re-think my plans a little. But fortunately I've managed to come up with a solution that I think both you and Dewbush here will find highly entertaining.'

'And what may that be?' asked Capstan, none the wiser.

'It would probably be easier if I just showed you.'

And with that, Morose pulled open the top drawer of his desk, and took out a handgun and a length of rope, laying each down carefully on the desk.

'Ah,' said Capstan, with sudden enlightenment, which was soon replaced by an overall feeling of primordial fear, mixed together with deep-rooted clinical depression.

Chapter Twenty Three
An elevating journey

17:01 BST

CLAIRE WAS LYING sprawled out on one of her uncle's angular-shaped black leather sofas, in the middle of his somewhat spacious executive office suite situated at the very top of the former HIGD Tower which was now called Number 10 Downing Street. She'd had an exhausting couple of days, but had been keen to pop in to let Robert know what had been going on, specifically in relation to the potential job offer from Sir John Safebusy.

'So, anyway,' she said, gazing up at the ceiling, 'Sir John said that I should come and work for them in some sort of a senior capacity.'

'That's nice,' said Robert, as he endeavoured to work out how to bcc someone on an email he was attempting to send.

'Probably as their PR Director, or maybe something in Advertising,' she continued.

'Oh, yes,' said Robert again.

'Which I'm sure would come with a very generous salary.'

'That's interesting.'

'And Carl, he's their Head of Marketing, says that all their senior staff get a free shopping account as one of the perks of the job!'

'Wow!' said Robert, doing his best to show genuine interest.

'And their Premier Range of ready meals really is quite excellent.'

Before she started to move on to the price of milk, or how many loyalty card points she'd need to get a free shopping trip to New York, Robert thought he'd better change the subject.

'So, how'd everything go on the Isle of Wight?'

'You mean, The People's Independent Republic of the Isle of Wight?'

'That isn't really what they've decided to call themselves, is it?'

'Uh-huh.'

'But doesn't it sound a little…left-wing?'

'I suppose, but I think they're looking to adopt a more communal approach to managing their economy, and probably thought that the name would help.'

'You mean communal as in…*sharing*?' asked Robert, struggling to say the one word that went against just about everything he'd ever stood for in his entire life.

'Something like that.'

'Or what is known in political terms as Communism!'

'Is it?' asked Claire.

'Which has been proven, time and time again, not to work.'

'Has it?'

'And it's the very first thing you learn when you enter politics. You simply can't run a successful market economy if everything's being *shared around* equally.'

'Well, it looks like they're going to try it out for a while.'

'And furthermore,' continued Robert, 'whoever ends up in charge eventually comes to the obvious realisation that they're better than everyone else, and so, *ipso facto*, deserve a lot more!'

'Do they?'

'You should get them to read George Orwell's *Animal Farm*. It's the most straightforward account of the inherent failings of the Communist system that's ever been written.'

'Is it?'

'If it was down to me, everyone on Planet Earth should be forced to read it.'

'And what about all those people who can't read?'

'As long as there's an audio version available, I can't see that as being a problem.'

'So, anyway,' said Claire, deciding to change the subject herself, 'they're confident that they'll be able to supply us with sufficient quantities of cannabis, to cover the initial uptake at least.'

'And what about Safebusy's?' asked Robert.

'It took a while, but Sir John is on board, and I've been told that he's already arranged an exclusive trading deal with the Isle of Wight, who are shipping out the first consignment tomorrow.'

'You mean, The People's Independent Republic of the Isle of Wight,' corrected Robert, with a sarcastic smirk.

Claire ignored him. 'And they've decided to launch with a basic below-the-line price promotion, instead of a TV ad. So they're pretty much all set to go and are just waiting for it to be officially legalised.'

'Looks like it's full steam ahead then!'

'But what about Parliament?' asked Claire.

'I pushed it through this afternoon, and I'll do the House of Lords tomorrow. And then I suggest you pick yourself up some Safebusy shares. I've a feeling they'll be going into orbit by the end of the week.'

Having given up trying to send the email, he turned his monitor off and looked over at Claire.

'How about I take you out for a celebratory drink?'

'I thought you'd never ask!'

'C'mon then! Let's get out of here, and before that idiot Private Secretary of mine turns up to tell me otherwise.'

But as they both heaved themselves out of their respective chairs, there was a knock on the door, followed by the entrance of the very man Robert was always keen to avoid.

'The Home Secretary's here to see you, Prime Minister,' announced Fredrick Overtoun.

'It's too late, Freddy, it's gone five o'clock, and I've already agreed to take my niece here out for a celebratory drink,'

'That's nice, Prime Minister, but he does say that it's rather urgent.'

'Really? That's a first. I'm not sure I've ever heard that one before.'

'He actually said that it's rather *very* urgent, Prime Minister, and he's already waiting for you, in the corridor.'

'If he *really* needs to talk to me, then he can do it in the lift on the way down. Did you hear that, Harold?'

Robert called out, as he could already see Harold Percy-Blakemore's crumpled little face peering at him from around the door.

'If you say so, Prime Minister, but as I just told Fredrick, it's extremely and most definitely *very urgent*, Prime Minister.'

'Well, you'd better press the button for the lift then, hadn't you?'

'Of course, Prime Minister.' His face disappeared back behind the door.

Turning to his niece, who was taking a moment to check her makeup, Robert said, 'C'mon, Claire, there's a bottle of Moët & Chandon Bi-Centenary Cuvée Dry Imperial 1943 waiting out there somewhere with our name on it, and the day certainly isn't getting any younger.'

'And neither am I. Give us a sec,' she muttered through pursed lips, as she finished re-applying her lipstick, before chasing after her uncle, who she discovered had already left the room.

'Goodbye, Freddy,' she said, breezing straight past him.

'Goodbye, Miss Bridlestock. Have a good evening.'

'I always do,' she said, looking back towards him, adding both a wink and a mischievous smile.

'HOLD THAT DOOR!' shouted Robert to Harold, who was waiting by a line of five elevators ahead of him. Harold did as he was told, while Robert and Claire stepped inside.

'Car Park Level Three please,' requested Robert, catching his breath.

'Yes, Prime Minister.' The Home Secretary ran his

finger down the forty-five buttons before landing on the one just above Car Park Level Two.

'And you have until then to discuss whatever it is that you want to talk to me about.'

'Yes, Prime Minister, and thank you.'

And as the lift began its smooth, gradual descent, but with nothing more being said by either Harold or anyone else, Robert prompted, 'Well then?'

'Well, er, what, Prime Minister?'

'We're not on a journey down to the centre of the earth, Harold. You do know that, don't you?'

'I'm sorry, Prime Minister, I'm not with you.'

'Let me put it another way. I believe there are only forty-two floors in total, excluding the three levels that make up the car park, and as you've only got until we reach the lobby, may I be so bold as to suggest that you get on with it?'

'Oh, of course. Sorry, Prime Minister. It's just that I've been sent a link to a YouTube video, which I thought you'd better see.'

'You want me to watch a video?'

'Er, yes, Prime Minister.'

'And that's what you consider to be "extremely and most definitely very urgent", is it?'

'It is, Prime Minister. And I have it on my new smartphone!' he announced, just as the elevator stopped at floor number Thirty-Nine, and the doors pinged open to let two more people in.

Harold turned on his phone, clicked on the link and held it up for Robert and Claire to see.

'It's apparently been filmed by the new Head of The Centre for Organised Crime and Kidnapping,' said Harold, by way of introduction, as they all started to watch an elliptical circle go around on itself signifying that the video had begun to load.

'Oh, you mean, COCK?' asked Robert.

The two people who'd just entered the lift glanced over their shoulders and gave Robert a peculiar look.

'Yes, Prime Minister, but we always like to refer to them as The Centre for Organised Crime and Kidnapping.'

'Yes, I know, but it's a bit of a mouthful, isn't it?'

'What, COCK is, Prime Minister?'

The two people in front smirked at each other, and as they both began to go bright red, thought it best to examine their feet for a while.

'No, you idiot!' said Robert. 'Having to say The Centre for Organised Crime and Kidnapping all the bloody time.'

'Oh, yes. Maybe, Prime Minister, but unfortunately the word COCK always comes across as being, well, a bit… er, inappropriate, Prime Minister.'

'I suppose,' said Robert, with general indifference, and looked again at the smartphone, but the loading circle was still going around on itself.

Feeling his patience begin to ebb away, he asked, 'When's this bloody video going to start?'

'Anytime now, Prime Minister. The reception is never all that great from up here.'

'As much as I enjoy watching things go around in endless circles,' said Robert, 'I don't! Can't you make it go any faster?'

'It's just coming up now, Prime Minister,' and as the lift stopped once again, this time to let three people in from floor number Thirty-Four, they all moved in a little to make more room as Harold raised the volume to just below full.

'GOOD NEWS!' boomed the sound of an over-excited professionally trained voice. 'THE YOUGET HALF-PRICE SUMMER SALE IS NOW ON!'

'Oh, sorry, Prime Minister, it's an advert,'

'ALL GARDEN FURNITURE, HALF-PRICE!'

'Can't you skip it?' asked Robert.

'GAZEBOS, HALF-PRICE!'

'I don't seem to be able to, Prime Minister.'

'BARBEQUES, HALF-PRICE!'

'Can you at least turn it down?'

'BADMINTON SETS, HALF-PRICE!'

'Oh, yes, of course.'

'CRICKET BATS, HALF-PRICE!'

'You're turning it up, Harold, not down!'

'BUT HURRY! LIKE THE BRITISH SUMMER, THE YOUGET HALF-PRICE SUMMER SALE WON'T LAST FOREVER!'

'Sorry, Prime Minister. It's a new phone, and I'm still getting used to it.'

'YOUGET! GET MORE, FOR LESS!'

'I've turned it down, Prime Minister.'

'Yes, but it's finished now, so you'd better turn it back up again.'

'Oh, right. Sorry. Hold on.'

And as Harold increased the volume once more, he held it up on its side so that Claire, Robert and he could all see its average-sized rectangular screen.

Looming into view came a giant of a man with a large bald head and a black beard that had the top lip shaved, so that it looked more like a half-beard. With the speaker coming up to full volume, they were able to begin listening to what he'd already started to say.

'*As you can see, we have the distinct pleasure of entertaining two brand new guests,*' said the over-sized man as he stood to one side to let his viewers see that he was in some sort of a walled courtyard that was completely deserted but for two men located in its very centre. They were sitting next to each other, with their hands behind their backs, on what looked to be some sort of a deluxe family sized barbeque, remarkably similar to the one that had just been featured on the YouGet advert.

The camera then followed the speaker as he began to lumber towards them, all the while continuing with his commentary.

'*That one sitting on the left, is the highly decorated Detective Inspector Andrew Capstan of the Solent Police, who not only has an OBE, but also two Queen's Police Medals for Gallantry and Distinguished Service!*'

As the camera came in closer, it was able to focus in on the first man who just scowled straight back with a look of general continental disgruntlement about him.

'*And that other one, the one with the gag on, is Dewbush.*'

The camera panned over to film the other man, who had a more cheerful countenance, and mumbled something that was either, '*Hello, Mum*', or '*My bum is numb,*' but with his mouth incapacitated by the gag it was difficult to tell which.

Just then the lift stopped again, and seven more people stepped in. The doors closed, the elevator continued its descent, and the commentator with the shaved head and beard-thing continued with his narration.

'You probably can't see this, but they're actually sitting on a Bondi-Barbie G4, which is generally considered to be the very best family barbeque on the market.'

The cameraman took a moment to film the appliance.

'And if you look underneath, you'll see we have not one, but three 13kg Propane gas bottles, and they've each got a kilogram of PE-4 Plastic Explosive taped onto the side.'

The Camera focused in on a YouGet price tag that said, "PE-4 Plastic Explosive, HALF-PRICE, ONLY £259.99."

'Now, this red and green wire here,' continued the larger than average man, as the camera followed the direction of his hand, *'leads to this YouGet alarm clock.'*

The camera moved in again as it tracked his fat white finger, all the way up to the top of one of the 13 kg Propane gas bottles where stood a harmless-looking digital radio alarm clock, into which the wires disappeared.

'I'm not sure if you'll be able to see this,' continued the speaker, *'but we've set it to go off at exactly ten o'clock tomorrow evening, just in time for the national evening news, and by which time one of two things will have happened.'*

The camera then pulled back from the clock to re-focus onto the narrator.

'Either you'll have allowed Flight 790 from Bogotá, Colombia, to land at Gatwick Airport at half-nine tomorrow evening, and its cargo to be unloaded without either being searched or confiscated by British Customs, or the PE-4 here will explode, along with these two fine-looking policeman.

'And in case you don't agree to our terms, we'll be running a live broadcast, starting at nine o'clock tomorrow night, right here on YouTube. I'm sure there will be many, many people throughout the UK, and probably even the World, who'd just love to watch a couple of British policeman being blown into several unidentifiable pieces.

'Anyway, the choice is yours, gentlemen,' and with that he gave the camera a wide grin, before seeming to remember to say, *'Oh, and you can call me at COCK's new Headquarters, right here at Portsmouth Prison, any time you like - the number's on the website - but preferably before bits of policeman start pebble-dashing the prison walls.'*

The video ended rather abruptly, and as Harold put away his smartphone, he asked, 'So, what do you think we should do, Prime Minister?'

'I'm not sure,' answered Robert. 'What do you think, Claire?'

The lift stopped again, this time at floor number nineteen, and as the doors pinged open, seven more people attempted to all push themselves in.

'Personally,' answered Claire, 'I think we should try to move up a bit.'

'I'd have to agree with Claire on that one,' said Robert. 'It's getting rather squashed-up in here.'

'I actually meant about the terrorists, Prime Minister?'

'I suppose we're just going to have to let their plane land, aren't we?'

'We are, Prime Minister?'

'Well, I for one am buggered if I'm going to let two innocent policeman be blown into a zillion pieces, just to stop a stupid plane from landing.'

'But surely, Prime Minister, we can't be seen by the world to be caving in to the demands of terrorists.'

'Why not? And besides, I'm quite unpopular enough without having a couple of our Boys in Blue murdered in cold blood, live on the news, especially when one of them's got an OBE. No! I suggest you give them a call and let them know that we're in full, total and absolute agreement.'

'And the plane, Prime Minister?'

'What about it?'

'What should we do when it lands, Prime Minister?'

'I've no idea, Harold. You're the Home Secretary. Maybe you should just keep an eye on it, in case it contains a nuclear weapon, or something worse.'

'Forgive me, Prime Minister, but what could possibly be *worse* than a nuclear weapon?' asked Harold, looking more worried than usual.

'I don't know, but possibly a Brazilian monkey carrying a 21st Century version of the Bubonic Plague, all set to wipe out the entire British population within just a few days?' suggested Robert.

Harold had to agree with him. That *was* worse than a nuclear bomb, and he began to watch the various people jammed in around him as they all breathed in and out which, to his current state of mind, seemed both unnecessary and potentially rather hazardous.

As the lift stopped at floor number eleven, and five more people pushed and shoved their way in, Robert asked, 'Is this the only lift in the entire building that's actually working?'

Grateful for the distraction, Harold answered, 'I think they all are, Prime Minister, it's just that it's gone five o'clock, so everyone's making their way home.'

'I'd better start leaving a little earlier then,' said Robert. 'I mean, this is just bloody stupid!'

'Yes, Prime Minister.'

'How many people can this thing safely hold, anyway?' asked Robert, looking around to see if there was some sort of a maximum capacity sign.

The sign in question was pressed up against Harold's face, and although he felt he already had enough to worry about, he pulled his head away, enough at least to be able to read it.

'It says it can hold up to twenty-one people, Prime Minister.'

'One, two, three, four,' counted Robert quietly to himself, as he began to tot up how many were already inside; and as he did, so did everyone else, but all with as much discretion as possible.

'I hate to be the bearer of bad news,' Robert announced moments later, and to all those crammed into the lift, 'but there are twenty-seven people in here already.'

Everyone began exchanging anxious glances with each other.

'What floor are we on?' asked Harold, who wasn't as tall as Robert and couldn't see from where he was standing.

'Just coming up to eight now,' answered Robert.

'So we're nearly there then?' asked Harold, seeking reassurance that if the elevator's cable was about to give way, they wouldn't have too far to drop.

'Yes, but there are still the three car park levels beneath the ground floor, so effectively we're still eleven floors up,' said Robert, who'd began bouncing up and down on the balls of his feet, which made the elevator wobble somewhat precariously each time he did so. Despite being forced into being in such close proximity to *normal* people, for some unknown reason he'd begun to find himself rather enjoying the experience.

But for everyone else, including Claire, what had been the very definition of a confined space was beginning to resemble a larger than average coffin, and sensing that they could probably all do with being cheered up, Robert asked, 'I don't suppose anyone knows any good jokes?'

His question was met by four walls of silence, along with an ominously quite floor, and a ceiling to which was attached a cable that had only been designed to support the weight of twenty-one averagely sized people, and all of which seemed to be closing in on them.

'Tell you what,' Robert continued, 'I'll go first.'

Claire, jammed up next to him, let out a loud and rather obvious groan. She must have heard his jokes at least a dozen times before, all two of them.

Ignoring her, Robert started.

'A horse walks into the bar and the barman says, "Why the long face?"'

Claire was first to show her lack of amusement. 'Do you have any idea how many times I've heard you tell that one?'

'Yes, but it's still good though!'

'I'm not even sure it is a joke! Aren't they supposed to involve some sort of a question, like, what's white and wears tartan trousers?'

'That's my Rupert the Bear joke!' Robert protested, clearly put out that she'd attempted to steal his very best one.

'I know a good one, Prime Minister,' said Harold, happy to have the opportunity to think about something other than a possible nuclear weapon being detonated directly underneath the Houses of Parliament, or a Brazilian monkey that, despite displaying all the symptoms of advanced Bubonic Plague, may be, at that precise moment in time, being waived through customs. Or even his current predicament of being forced to stand inside a dangerously over-crowded elevator that was still about a hundred feet above where he'd have preferred it to be.

'Really?' asked Robert, somewhat surprised. He'd never heard his Home Secretary tell a joke before. Not even at the Cabinet Office Christmas Party, where he was known for wandering around, completely drunk, with his tackle hanging out, along with his trouser pockets, doing a remarkably convincing impression of a baby elephant.

Having given it a little more thought, Harold said, 'I think so, Prime Minister.'

'Well, what is it then?'

He took a deep breath and said, 'Why can't a bicycle stand up on its own?'

'I don't know. Why can't a bicycle stand up on its own?' asked Robert, as he felt obliged to.

'Because it's *too tired*!' exclaimed Harold, adding a broad grin to help sell the punchline.

The elevator fell into a muted silence, and after a few moments, Claire spoke up saying, 'I'm sorry, but I don't get it.'

'I'm not sure there's anything to get,' added Robert.

'It's funny,' explained Harold, 'because a bicycle's got two tyres. But "two tyres" sounds almost exactly the same as *too tired*.'

Just then, the lift stopped, and as the doors pinged open, everyone let out a sigh of relief, apart from Harold. He was disappointed that nobody had laughed at his joke. However, he'd reached the lobby, and as everyone else had already squeezed their way out, he found himself alone, with just Robert and Claire for company, who both still had to go down one more floor to Car Park Level 3. So he thought he'd better be off and said, 'See you tomorrow then, Prime Minister.'

Robert responded in the same way he always did whenever one of his Cabinet Ministers had the misfortune to say goodbye to him, and asked, 'Do I have to?'

But Harold knew that Robert was only being his normal jocular self, and added a 'Cheerio', along with a wave, before stepping out of the lift and into Number 10 Downing Street's vast, opulent, marble-clad lobby.

As the doors closed, leaving Robert and Claire on their own again, Robert said, 'I really think we need to lay down some ground rules about who owns which joke.'

'Well,' said Claire, 'as I now know both of yours, I suggest we share them.'

'You know that I don't do that. We'd better take one each.'

'Only if I can have the Rupert the Bear one.'

'No! You can have the one about the horse. The Rupert the Bear joke is definitely mine! Agreed?' He turned towards her with his right hand extended.

'Agreed!' said Claire, and took his proffered hand.

Giving it a vigorous shake, Robert smiled victoriously at her, adding, 'And no swap-backs!' just in case she changed her mind.

Chapter Twenty Four
You'll never get away with it

Wednesday, 29th July
21:54 BST

KEEN TO ENSURE that Flight 790 from Bogotá, Colombia, along with its consignment of premium grade cocaine that he'd bought through his old police contact, Doctor "Charlie" Lactose, Head of Portsmouth Hospital's Accident and Emergency Department, landed safely at Gatwick Airport without being either shot down or having its consignment impounded, Morose had decided to attend in person by sneaking out of Portsmouth Prison. He'd been able to do this, along with a hand-picked selection of his men, without the surrounding press pack or anyone else noticing, by simply driving straight out of the prison's main gates disguised as YouGet delivery men. This wasn't as difficult as it may have sounded, as they still had the four vans from their felonious adventures on Monday night, and the sight of YouGet vans driving around the country was common enough for nobody to raise so much as an eyebrow, even if there were four of them, all driving out at the same time, one after another.

He'd decided to take Capstan and Dewbush along

with him as well, so they'd been shoved into the back of the one he'd been driving, and were only separated from him by a security wire mesh, enabling him to keep a close eye on them.

Furthermore, just in case the British Government decided to do a U-turn, as they were known to, he'd brought along the same deluxe family barbeque set, the 13kg Propane gas bottles, the 3kg of PE-4 Plastic Explosive, the digital radio alarm clock, the prison camcorder, and the former Warden's Wi-Fi-enabled laptop.

Squeezed in behind the wheel, Morose was now parked up to watch from a relatively safe distance as his fittest and strongest men transferred the contents of the Columbian Air's Lockheed Martin C-130 Hercules into the three other YouGet vans. They were doing so at quite a pace, as they were being watched over by dozens of Customs officials and numerous policemen who stood beside their cars as the flashing blue lights whirled silently around, all desperately hoping to receive the order to move in and arrest the lot of them.

As he watch the vans being loaded, he called back, 'As you can probably see,' speaking more loudly than normal to ensure that Capstan and Dewbush could hear him from where they were, tied up in the back along with the barbeque, the propane gas canisters and the explosives, 'my men have nearly finished loading the vans with what I've been assured is the highest quality cocaine on the international market. And I reckon that in just a few days, once I've posted a couple of hundred thousand free samples to the population of Portsmouth, and because of its somewhat "moreish" nature, I'll have created an almost overnight demand. And I'll then be able to roll it out to the rest of the UK, and maybe even the world. What do you think about that, Capstan?'

Capstan really couldn't give a shit. All he cared about was getting as far away from Morose and his "Barbeque of Death" as possible, and with that at the forefront of his mind, called out, 'YOU'LL NEVER GET AWAY WITH IT!'

Capstan had been taught to use that phrase during his Graduate Fast Track Police Training Programme, but knowing that Morose would have also been taught to use the exact same phrase, decided *not* to use it for the purpose in which it was intended, which was to try to discourage a criminal from being able to get away with it. No! Capstan had used it to actively *encourage* Morose to do his very best to try and get away with it, and subsequently for him to become so absorbed by the process that he wouldn't think to look behind him to see how Capstan and Dewbush were getting on. And that was because, during the one hour twenty minute journey up to Gatwick Airport, they'd managed to work in silent co-operation, which was a first, and had very nearly been able to untie each other's restraints.

'Oh, I think I will get away with it,' retorted Morose. 'In fact, it looks like they're nearly finished loading up the vans, so I'm probably not only going to get away with it, but I'm going to get away with *all* of it!' He couldn't help himself and let out a deranged sort of a laugh.

'I REALLY DON'T THINK YOU WILL!' called out Capstan again, who could feel that he was very nearly free, and just needed a minute or two longer.

'But why, Capstan? Why won't I get away with it?'

'YOU JUST WON'T, THAT'S ALL!' said Capstan, as Dewbush was able to free his wrists from the final knot.

'I know the police teach you to say "You'll never get away with it", Capstan, but in this case it just doesn't make any sense. After all, I have the men, I have the vans, and now it looks like I have the cocaine. So all I need now is to buy two-hundred thousand second class stamps and some manila envelopes.'

But just then, Morose heard something behind him that sounded very much like the double van doors being gently closed. In his offside rear-view mirror he glimpsed Capstan and Dewbush attempting to make a run for it, into the blackness of the surrounding night.

Cursing the fact that he'd not bothered to lock the rear doors, he involuntarily made an effort to leap out to stop them, but then remembered that he weighed well over two hundred kilograms, and couldn't think of the last time he'd been able to leap anywhere. So he decided to simply let them go. After all, the last YouGet van had just finished being loaded, and he could already see his men securing its rear doors. He didn't need them anymore.

Then he heard a commotion up ahead, followed by the sound of more van doors being opened and closed. A plume of thick black diesel smoke erupted from the nearest van as it nearly reversed over the men who were still standing behind it, before doing an impressive wheel spin and driving off.

Winding down his window, Morose called out, 'WHAT THE HELL'S GOING ON?'

'It's those two policeman, Gov,' said one of the men who'd nearly been driven over. 'They've just nicked one of our vans!'

'WELL, WHAT ARE YOU WAITING FOR? GET AFTER THEM!'

'But - but that was the van we came up in, Gov!'

Ignoring him, Morose shouted, 'THE REST OF YOU, DON'T LET THEM GET AWAY!' As others began clambering into the remaining YouGet vans, the two who'd had their vehicle stolen looked over at Morose, clearly hoping for a lift.

'ALL RIGHT!' shouted Morose, giving in to his better nature. 'JUMP IN, BUT HURRY!'

'Yes, Gov,' they said, and pelted towards the passenger-side door.

The last man finished climbing in. Catching his breath, he said, 'They'll never get away with this, Gov!'

'Well, they're doing a pretty fucking good job of it so far,' replied Morose. 'Now put your seat belts on and shut the fuck up!'

As Morose's YouGet van rumbled into life, along with the numerous police cars who'd all been ordered to follow the fleet of vans once they'd been loaded up with whatever had been in the plane, they all set off after Inspector Capstan, Sergeant Dewbush, and the YouGet van that was crammed to the roof with premium grade cocaine that they'd decided to commandeer in order to make an effective get-away themselves.

Chapter Twenty Five
A testing drive

22:12 BST

HOLDING ON TO the steering wheel as if his life depended on it, and with his heart pounding deep inside his chest, Dewbush asked, 'Where are we headed, Sir?' while giving his offside rear-view mirror a furtive glance.

'Just follow the signs for the M23—heading south,' said Capstan, between breaths. 'The signposts will probably be for Brighton. I'll see if I can dig out a map, but if we can make it to the Solent Police Station, I reckon we'll be safe.'

'There's a whole convoy chasing after us, Sir!'

Capstan took the opportunity to glance into his own side-view mirror, where he could see three other YouGet vans in hot pursuit, closely followed by what seemed to be an endless number of police cars, all with sirens blaring and blue lights flashing.

'I suggest you don't look back, Dewbush. Just keep your eyes focussed on the road ahead.'

'I'll try, Sir,' said Dewbush, as he leaned forward, so that he was peering over the top of the steering wheel.

'Look!' said Capstan. 'There's a sign for the M23. Just follow that, and whatever you do, don't go the wrong way!'

'How'd you mean, Sir?'

'We need to go South, Dewbush, SOUTH! Not up to bloody London!'

'Yes, Sir. I'll do my best, Sir.'

'Don't do your best, Dewbush! Just don't drive us up north, else we'll be here all bloody day!'

'Yes, Sir. I'll try, Sir.'

'OK, stay in this lane, but *watch out for that SPEEDBUMP!*

Dewbush hadn't seen it, and as they were pushing fifty-five in a thirty zone, they hit it hard, momentarily lifting the entire van off the ground to land five feet beyond with a hefty thud.

Dewbush fought hard to bring the van back under control, and as soon as it had stopped lurching from side to side rather dramatically, apologised. 'Sorry about that, Sir, but I think we're still in one piece.'

Capstan was too busy putting his seatbelt on to think what choice words of condemnation he could use to berate his sergeant.

A quick glance into his rear-view side mirror told Capstan that one of the YouGet vans behind them hadn't faired so well, and must have lost control when they'd hit the same bump, as it had driven straight into a lamppost with such force that the streetlamp itself had exploded.

'We've managed to lose one, Dewbush!'

'A police one, or a YouGet one, Sir?' asked Dewbush, attempting to see for himself in his side-view mirror.

'It was one of the vans, but keep your eyes on the

road!'

'Yes, Sir.'

A few moments later they both began to realise that it was becoming increasingly difficult to see out through the window, which was odd, as it was a clear, cloudless night without a wisp of fog. But it didn't take them long to work out why.

'It's getting terribly dusty in here, Sir,' mentioned Dewbush.

'Yes, I know,' agreed Capstan, tasting something peculiar in his mouth. 'Hitting that speedbump must have split open one of the sacks in the back. I'd better put the air conditioning on, to help clear the air.'

As Capstan did that, he pushed on with providing Dewbush with directions.

'There's another sign coming up,' he said, as he endeavoured to peer out. 'OK, get into the right-hand lane and follow the road around.'

'Your right or my right, Sir?'

'We both have the same right, Dewbush!'

'Forgive me, Sir, but I write with my left hand, so my left is probably your right.'

Capstan paused momentarily as he tried to work that one out, but soon realised that it made absolutely no sense whatsoever, and stared over at his intellectually challenged subordinate.

'What the fuck are you talking about, Dewbush?'

'I'm just saying, Sir, that I'm left-handed, and so I write with my left hand.'

'And what's that got to do with anything?'

'Well, Sir, it means that my left is, in effect, your right, Sir.'

'Are you trying to wind me up, Sergeant?'

'Er, of course not, Sir.'

'Look, just stay in the right-hand lane, will you, before I kick you out and drive the van myself!'

'But, which...er?'

'THAT SIDE, DEWBUSH! THAT SIDE! THAT SIDE!' shouted Capstan, frantically pointing at the right side of the road.

'Yes, Sir, but there's really no need to shout.'

'I wouldn't have to if you knew your left from your right, for fuck's sake! I mean, how on God's earth you ever managed to pass your driving test is beyond me.'

'I haven't taken it yet, Sir.'

'What do you mean, you haven't taken it yet?'

'I've got a Provisional Licence, Sir, so I've never had to.'

'I don't believe this,' said Capstan, as he double-checked that his seatbelt buckle was locked in securely.

'I joined the police straight out of school, Sir,' continued Dewbush, feeling it necessary to offer some sort of an explanation, 'and as I've never needed my own car, I've never had to pass my test, Sir.'

'But - but,' said Capstan, momentarily lost for words. 'But...you're not allowed to drive *any* car on a Provisional License, Dewbush!'

'Oh, I'm fairly sure that I am, Sir, as long as I'm with a passenger who holds a full one. And as I'm normally driving with you, Sir, I haven't felt it necessary to take my test. And besides, Sir, lessons are really expensive!'

Under any other circumstances, Capstan would have ordered Dewbush to stop the van to change places, but given the fact that they were still being pursued by two YouGet vans and more police cars than he could count, he decided to let it go, for now, and re-focussed on making sure that they were headed in the right direction.

'OK, we're merging on to the M23, Dewbush. Just keep going and I'll look out for a sign for Portsmouth.'

'Right you are, Sir.'

Another glance into his side-view mirror told Capstan that all the vehicles behind them were definitely closing in.

'Can't this thing go any faster, Dewbush?'

'Probably, Sir, but the motorway speed limit is seventy.'

'I think we can forgo the speed limit on this occasion, Dewbush.'

'Are you sure, Sir?'

'Just floor the bloody thing, will you?'

Yes, Sir,' he said, and a moment later, 'my foot's hard on the floor now, Sir.'

'Good! How fast are we going?'

'Seventy-one, Sir.'

Another quick look into the mirror confirmed Capstan's suspicions.

'We're just too heavy, Dewbush. We're going to have to get rid of that stuff in the back.'

'What, you mean the cocaine, Sir?'

'Yes, Dewbush,' said Capstan, feeling his teeth beginning to itch.

'But how, Sir? It's been loaded up to the roof! The only way to get it out would be through the wire mesh, Sir, and to do that we'd need something like a teaspoon, which I reckon would take a fair while, Sir, and I'm not even sure we've got one.'

'You're just going to have to climb out, Dewbush, and make your way to the rear doors.'

There was a lull in the conversation as Dewbush attempted to digest that new order, and what exactly it could mean for his future wellbeing.

'But who's going to drive, Sir?' he eventually asked.

'I will,' answered Capstan. 'And anyway, you shouldn't even be behind the wheel!'

'So, you want me to get out, Sir, climb onto the roof, make my way to the back of the van, undo the doors and then... What? Throw the cocaine out the back, Sir?'

'Exactly, Dewbush, and see if you can hit one of those YouGet vans whilst you're at it. Preferably the one being driven by that mass-murdering psychotic nut-job, Morose!'

Dewbush inverted his lips to use the outside of them to rub against his teeth, before saying, 'No problem. Shall I go now, Sir?'

'Yes, please, Sergeant.'

'Right you are, Sir,' and placing one hand on the door latch, asked, 'Are you ready to take the wheel, Sir?'

'I've got that. Now, try and keep your foot on the accelerator for as long as possible. As soon as you're out, I'm going to use my stick to keep the pedal pushed down.'

'And you'll be able to steer at the same time, will you, Sir?'

'Piece of cake, Dewbush.'

Feeling very much like he could take over the world armed only with an assortment of Liquorice Allsorts, Dewbush undid the latch and started to force it open, which wasn't easy due to the speed of the air being pushed against it from the outside. Capstan held the wheel with his left hand, hovering his stick over Dewbush's foot with his right, ready to take over.

When Dewbush was nearly all the way out he called back, 'SHALL I TAKE MY FOOT OFF NOW, SIR?'

'YES, DEWBUSH, TAKE IT OFF NOW!'

'RIGHT YOU ARE, SIR,' and as his leg disappeared out of the van, and the door was forced closed, Capstan jammed down hard on the pedal with his walking stick and focussed on keeping the van steering straight, as they continued south, down the M23.

A few minutes later, Capstan heard the sound of one of the rear doors being opened.

'I'VE MADE IT, SIR!' came Dewbush's voice from the very back of the van.

'WELL DONE, DEWBUSH! NOW START THROWING ALL THAT COCAINE OUT!'

'RIGHT YOU ARE, SIR!'

Out of the corner of his eye, in the driver's side-view mirror, Capstan began to see sack-shaped objects flying out from the back of the van and exploding onto the motorway in giant white balls of dust. Keeping his stick firmly pressed against the foot pedal, he flicked his eyes over to the speedometer's needle to see that it had already crept up, and was now registering just over seventy-five.

'Good work, Dewbush,' he said to himself, and re-focussed on doing his part by keeping the van as steady and as straight as he could.

It wasn't long before Dewbush was able to throw most of the cargo out, and had reached the wire mesh, behind where Capstan was.

'I've nearly...finished,' he said, struggling for breath, 'and I even managed to hit...one of the YouGet Vans...and they went flying off..., Sir...into the hard shoulder.'

'Well done, Dewbush. Really well done!'

'Thank you, Sir. So...there's only one YouGet van left now, Sir....but it's the one being driven by...Morose.'

'Never mind, Dewbush. You've done all that could be expected of you.'

'How are we doing for speed, Sir?'

'Just over eighty-five.'

'That's good, Sir,' and having managed to get his breath back, asked, 'Shall I climb back around?'

'If you could, Dewbush. And if you could close the back doors again, I think it would help with the aerodynamics.'

'Yes, Sir. I'll just throw these last few sacks out, Sir, and then I'll make my way back.'

It wasn't long before Capstan heard the rear doors close and shortly after that for Dewbush's head to appear at the driver's side window, which he knocked on, smiling and waving at his boss.

Unable to return the gesture, Capstan just nodded, and gesticulated for him to climb back in. So Dewbush forced open the driver's door and squeezed himself through the gap, taking hold of the wheel as he did so.

He exchanged Capstan's stick with his right foot, sat back down, pulled the door closed and put his seat belt on.

'Good work again, Dewbush. Highly commendable!'

'Thank you, Sir. I actually quite enjoyed it. And look, Sir, we're doing over ninety!'

But as Capstan took a moment to see who was left behind them, he heard the van's indicator clicking on and off.

'Where the hell do you think you're going, Dewbush?'

'We've nearly run out of petrol, Sir, but don't worry, there's a service station just up ahead.'

Capstan glanced over to see that the fuel gauge was indeed well into the red, and resigned himself to the fact that they were just going to have to give up.

'Oh well, Dewbush, we gave it our best shot, and besides, I could do with stretching my legs.'

'Me too, Sir, and I really wouldn't mind a coffee, Sir. And something to eat, perhaps.'

'I know what you mean, Sergeant. But at least we were able to unload all that cocaine, and with those police cars behind us, hopefully Morose will just leave us alone and continue on down to Portsmouth.'

'He is, Sir,' confirmed Dewbush, who'd already turned off the motorway to head up the slip road towards the service station, and could see that Morose's YouGet van wasn't following behind.

'Well, that's a relief, Dewbush. I think a celebratory coffee and a sandwich is definitely in order, don't you?'

'Actually, Sir, I wouldn't mind a Red Bull instead.'

'A coffee and a Red Bull it is!' said Capstan, feeling remarkably upbeat. 'Tell you what. If you fill her up, I'll pop in to get the drinks and the sandwiches, and then I can pay for the petrol whilst I'm there.'

However, although Morose had indeed continued down the M23, every other police car had made up their mind to follow on after the leading van, especially as it seemed to have been deliberately throwing sacks crammed full of what was either flour or Class A drugs at them. So, before Capstan and Dewbush had even pulled up beside the petrol pumps, over thirty police cars swarmed into the service station with sirens screaming and with scant regard for either speed limits or the safety of all those onlookers who'd stopped dead in their tracks to film the event with their smartphones.

'*GET OUT OF THE VAN WITH YOUR HANDS UP!*' bellowed the policeman who'd managed to beat all his colleagues to it.

'Do they mean us?' asked Dewbush.

'I suspect they probably do, Dewbush. But don't worry. We have our police identifications on us this time, so as long as you let me do all the talking, I'm sure we'll be fine.'

Chapter Twenty Six
Putting things into perspective

Thursday, 30th July
10:15 BST

'YOUR NEW TELESCOPE'S arrived, Prime Minister, as have the morning papers.'

Robert, having just put his feet up on the desk, lifted them off again, and retrieved his coffee.

'Excellent news, Freddy. Really excellent news!'

Assuming that he must have been referring to the arrival of the telescope, and not the papers, Robert's Private Secretary could only think to say, 'Er, yes, Prime Minister.'

'Well? Where is it then?'

'I thought it might be better if we went through the papers first, Prime Minister.'

'That's fascinating, Freddy. No, really, it is. Now if you can pop out and find the telescope, I'll do my upmost not to demote you down to Car Park Attendant.'

Fredrick had been expecting a response similar to that, although he hadn't predicted the raising of the subject of his continued employment as the Prime Minister's Private Secretary, so wasted no time in saying, 'It's in the hall, Prime Minister.'

'Good man. Bring it in and we can start setting it up.'

Placing his pile of newspapers on top of Robert's desk, Fredrick dutifully said, 'Yes, Prime Minister,' and stepped out of the office.

'It's a fair size!' exclaimed Robert, who'd decided to hold the door open for Fredrick so that he could watch it being carried in.

'Where would you like it, Prime Minister?' asked Fredrick, hoping it would be somewhere close by, being that it weighed at least half a tonne and he wasn't used to doing anything more strenuous than opening the occasional door.

'Over in the corner,' answered Robert, who was enjoying watching his Private Secretary do some real work for a change.

'Which corner is that, Prime Minister?'

'That one, over there,' said Robert, pointing towards the far right-hand side.

Fredrick sighed to himself and began weaving his way over to where he was being directed.

'Actually no,' said Robert. 'Let's put it over on this side first. I'd like to have a look at London before I see if I can find my golf course.'

'Of course...Prime Minister,' answered Fredrick, struggling for breath as he staggered over to the opposite side.

Just as he reached the other window, Robert said, 'Sorry, Freddy. Scratch that. I'd better try and find my golf course first. They're supposed to be cutting back the trees along the seventeenth fairway today, and I want to make sure they don't fuck the whole thing up.'

By then, Fredrick was in danger of passing out, so he set it down where it was, and said, 'May I propose…Prime Minister…that you take a look at London first…just until I get my breath back?'

'You really must take better care of yourself, Freddy. At the rate you're going you'll be dead by the time you hit forty. Why don't you join a gym, or something?'

Bent over on his knees as he gasped for air, Fredrick eventually said, 'I'll certainly give the idea…my fullest consideration. Thank you…Prime Minister.'

'No problem, Freddy. Any time.' He studied the generously-proportioned telescope that was perched on three wonky legs. 'So, how does this thing work?'

'I think you look down it…Prime Minister,' answered Fredrick, with an almost indiscernible hint of sarcasm.

Fortunately for Fredrick, Robert didn't pick up on it.

'I meant, how do you set it up so that I *can* look down it?'

Regaining control of his breathing, enough at least to stand up straight, Fredrick rested one hand on top of the telescope and used the other to adjust the tripod underneath, so that each leg was evenly spread out, and having successfully completed that task, reached forward to remove the lens cap.

'I think it should be operational now, Prime Minister, and you can use this knob here to focus.'

As Robert began rubbing his hands together with expectant glee, his desk phone burbled into life.

'Get that for me Freddy, will you please?'

'Yes, Prime Minister.' Fredrick dragged himself over to the Prime Minister's desk to take the call. 'It's the Governor of the Bank of England, Prime Minister. Björn Schenken-Fraggen.'

'What the hell does he want?'

'I'm not sure, Prime Minister. Would you like me to ask him?'

'No. Just put him on speaker phone.'

'Of course, Prime Minister,' he said, and, a press of a button later, 'The Prime Minister's on the phone for you now, Mr Schenken-Fraggen.'

'*Are you there, Prime Minister?*'

'I'm here, Björn,' answered Robert, raising his voice enough to carry over to his desk. 'How can I help?'

'*I suppose you've read the papers?*'

'Of course,' lied Robert, with professional ease.

'*What on earth were you thinking?*' asked Björn, with a clear edge to his voice.

'I'm not exactly sure what you're referring to, Björn, but it's an unfortunate part of my daily routine to always give the newspapers a courtesy glance.'

'*No, Prime Minister, I meant about having cannabis legalised?*'

'Oh, yes. And what about it?'

'*May I ask who persuaded you to do such a thing?*'

'It was actually my idea, Björn. I've decided to become more of a People's Prime Minister. And the People wanted it legalised, so I did!'

'*Are you completely mad?*'

'Er, not that I'm aware of, Björn, but I really don't care for the tone of your voice!'

'Forgive me, Prime Minister, but…have you any idea why cannabis has been a banned substance in just about every country throughout the world since, well, since it was first discovered?'

'Short-sighted bureaucracy, no doubt,' answered Robert.

'An insightful understanding of the market economy, more like!' corrected the Governor of the Bank of England.

'Sorry, Björn, but I'm not with you.'

'Do you have any idea what the side effects of smoking cannabis are, Prime Minister?'

'Peaceful serenity followed by a compelling need to vote for the person who legalised it?' asked Robert, who'd never been anywhere near the stuff and subsequently hadn't a clue.

'It removes every human desire to do absolutely anything apart from eat food, have sex and talk bollocks, Prime Minister.'

'Does it?' asked Robert, wondering why nobody had told him that before, and ambled over towards his desk to make a note for Fredrick to pick some up for him.

'Like, going to work in order to pay the mortgage, for example, Prime Minister.'

'Really?' questioned Robert, a little confused as to the direct relationship between wanting to have sex all the time and monthly mortgage repayments.

'Yes, really, Prime Minister, and due to the fact that it's now on sale at Safebusy's, NOBODY'S BOTHERING TO SHOW UP FOR WORK, Prime Minister!'

'Now I'm sorry, Björn, but that simply isn't true. I'm here, and so's my Private Secretary. And I saw loads of people on my way in.'

'Let me be more precise, Prime Minister: nobody who lives beyond their means on a regular basis, or in other words, everyone in the UK under the age of thirty, which unfortunately includes the British Banking Elite, hardly any of whom have bothered to show up today. And because of that, the FTSE 100 is in freefall with 16 billion pounds having been wiped off the British stock market since they opened for trading!'

'Is that a lot?' asked Robert.

'Well, it's quite a lot, Prime Minister.'

'Okay, well, I can't turn back the clock, Björn, so I suggest you suspend trading for a while. And besides, it's probably just a minor blip. I suspect they'll all wake up tomorrow only to discover that they've run out of condoms, and that they'd promised to take their girlfriend out for lunch, in Paris, preferably in a new dress, and a new car, and will therefore be back at work in no time.'

Björn knew that Robert was right, but it was hardly the point.

'That may be so, Prime Minister, but may I be so bold as to ask that in the future, before major legislative changes are introduced that could have an adverse effect on the British economy, I be kept in the loop a little more?'

'No problem, Björn. Now if you don't mind, I really am rather busy.'

'Of course, Prime Minister, but if the same thing happens tomorrow, we'll need to discuss this matter with some urgency.'

'Yes, yes, yes, and I'd expect nothing less,' said Robert, and hung up the phone.

'Twat!' he said, to no one in particular. 'Right, where were we?'

'We were about to go through the national

newspapers, Prime Minister.'

'Very droll, Fredrick. Very droll.' He strolled back to his brand new toy.

Standing behind the over-sized telescope, he swivelled it down towards all the people who seemed to be wandering aimlessly around Canary Wharf, exactly where he felt they should be, about six hundred and fifty feet beneath him.

Bending his knees so that he could peer down at them, he exclaimed, 'My God! This is absolutely bloody amazing!'

'Yes, Prime Minister,' agreed Fredrick, as he felt he should.

'You can see *everything*!'

'No doubt, Prime Minister.'

'And there are some absolute corkers down there!'

'Is that so, Prime Minister?'

'There's one staring at her iPhone, smoking something, and I can see all the way down her bra!'

'That's nice, Prime Minister.'

'They're more than nice, Freddy. They're a joyful bounty of succulent goodness!'

'I'm sure they are,' said Fredrick, as he wondered if it would be worth trying to find a new employer by leaking the story to the Guardian that the current Prime Minister was nothing more than a lecherous pervert, who'd just spend over £5,000 on the most powerful portable telescope on the market, simply for the voyeuristic pleasure of staring down young ladies' tops as they passed underneath his office, from the forty-second floor of the brand new Number 10 Downing Street.

'She's sending someone a text,' Robert narrated.

'And I assume that you won't be trying to read it, Prime Minister.'

'Oh, shut up, Freddy! Hold on. Let me just focus in a little more. There we go. It says… "I've just bought some of that new Fair Trade Marijuana from Safebusy's".'

There was a momentary pause, as Robert waited for her to tap out the rest. '"And now I'm feeling so horny… that I think I'd fuck the first man who said hello."'

Robert took his eye away from the lens, blinked a few times, and stared back down again. She was still there, taking a pull on what he assumed must be a marijuana cigarette, as she continued to watch the screen, probably waiting for a response. A moment later it came through.

'Someone's replied, Freddy.'

'Really, Prime Minister.'

Re-adjusting the focus again, he started to read out what he could see.

'"L O L. Give me a call when he does, and we'll make it a threesome."'

Robert looked away from the lens and blinked again, and with his heart picking up a couple of additional beats, said, 'Have you got your mobile phone with you?'

'Er, yes, Prime Minister. I've always got my mobile phone with me.'

'Right! Good! Keep an eye on that girl down there for me. The one smoking the joint, with the black ponytail and the low-cut yellow dress. And whatever you do, *don't* let her out of your sight!'

'May I enquire as to why, Prime Minister?' asked Fredrick, as Robert raced over to his desk to retrieve his keys and mobile from out of the top drawer.

'I'm going to introduce myself, of course! I can't remember the last time I had a threesome, and I'm certainly not going to let this opportunity pass me by!'

Chapter Twenty Seven
Holiday plans

10:28 BST

MOROSE HADN'T slept well, and he'd woken up in an even worse mood than he'd been in when he'd gone to bed. At least then he'd been relieved to have made it back to base without having his van hit by a sack of cocaine, which could have easily forced him into the hard shoulder which, in turn, could have detonated the 3kg of P-4 Plastic Explosive that he'd had in the back, along with the Propane gas canisters and the family-sized barbeque.

Having been forced to have frozen pepperoni pizza for breakfast, again, as that was all they had left, along with a cup of instant coffee that seemed to taste worse with each one he had, Morose was pacing up and down on top of the prison's battlements with his hands buried deep in his pockets, staring down at his feet as he considered his next move, with only his personal bodyguards, Bazzer and Gazzer, for company.

Thanks to Inspector Capstan's inability to deliver ice-cream on time, he'd had to sacrifice all his prison guard hostages, and with Capstan's help again, he'd now lost his shipment of cocaine. But he still had his YouGet advanced military weaponry, along with a van, and a prison full of loyal volunteers.

He wasn't beaten yet!

What he needed to think of was some way to exact his revenge, not only on the society that had taken away his former life as a well-paid, highly respected Police Chief Inspector, but also on Inspector Capstan and that moronically inept sergeant of his, who'd managed to screw up his plans in very much the same way as they used to do with every case that he'd ever had the misfortune to give them.

He stopped for a moment, leaned his hands on the battlement walls and gazed out over the Solent. There must be something he could do to get his own back, but for the life of him, he couldn't think what.

'You should take a 'oliday, Gov,' suggested Bazzer, who was standing next to Gazzer as they both listened to their boss mutter, *Fucking Capstan,'* repeatedly under his breath. 'That would cheer you up.' He never liked to see his employers upset, and always did whatever he could to lift their spirits, and although that normally involved eliminating whoever was causing the problem, preferably with an axe, it wasn't unusual for him to offer the odd helpful suggestion. Morose didn't respond. 'I took one once'.

'What, a 'oliday?' asked Gazzer.

'Yeah, one of 'em.'

'Did you go anywhere nice?'

As Gazzer had started his own prison sentence for multiple murder at the tender age of sixteen, he'd never had a chance to go on holiday before; and that also meant that he'd never known anyone else who had gone on one either. But he'd seen enough repeat episodes of EastEnders to know that you were supposed to ask if they'd been anywhere nice, whenever someone told you that they'd just come back from one.

'Not really,' answered Bazzer.

There was a lull in the conversation, before Bazzer decided to continue. 'It was before I got banged up in here, of course.'

'Must've been,' said Gazzer.

'I went over to France.'

'On the ferry?'

'Nah. On one of those sailing boat type things. You know, the ones with the sails, and the boat.'

'Oh,' said Gazzer, with nothing more than passing interest. 'Was it any good?'

'It was alright, I s'pose,' replied Bazzer, 'But they kept making me do weird stuff all the time.'

'What, like porno type stuff?' asked Gazzer, becoming considerably more interested.

'Nah! Nuffin' like that.'

'Like what then?'

'When we got out to sea, they told me to lie down on the floor, in the bottom of the boat, like, and they kept callin' me Ballast all the time.'

'That's just so fucked up,' said Gazzer, which was what he always said when he found himself stuck for words.

'And when we'd nearly got there, they said that I'd done so well that I'd been promoted up to the position of Fender, and that's when they's hung me over the side and used me to stop the boat from crashin' into the harbour wall.'

'Seriously fucked up,' said Gazzer, again.

'And cus of that, I had to spend the night in a French hospital thing, cus I'd broken half me ribs. But the very next mornin' I was told to get back on the boat and do it again, all the way back to Portsmouth!'

Bazzer seemed to have finished; and after taking a couple of minutes to reflect on the story, Gazzer said, 'You know, that don't sound all that bad.' And to him, it really didn't.

Gazzer had spent much of his youth being physically tortured by his two elder brothers, which was how he'd ended up in prison. The day after he'd turned sixteen he'd beaten, stabbed and then shot his elder siblings until they were most definitely dead, but he'd only done so because his dad had bought him a knuckle-duster, a baseball bat, a kitchen knife, and a gun for his birthday, and he couldn't think what else to do with them.

'S'pose,' answered Bazzer. 'And the lying at the bottom of the boat bit was fine. But by the time we got back the weather had turned, and after being promoted up to Fender again, I had to spend three weeks in A&E. And they didn't even bovver to say thanks!'

Listening in on their conversation, Morose decided to keep his mouth shut. As a keen sailor himself, he wasn't sure if Bazzer was talking about one of the trips he'd taken over to France, and now that he thought about it, his bodyguard's face did ring a vague sort of a bell.

'Maybe you could go to the Isle of Wight, Gov?' suggested Gazzer.

'What was that?' asked Morose, as if awoken from a deep hypnotic state.

'You could go to the Isle of Wight, Gov. For a 'oliday, like. You could even nick one of those boats from the harbour, and me and Bazzer could be your crew!'

Morose stared out at the island that he could clearly see, shimmering on the horizon in the bright morning sunshine. Then he gazed over towards Portsmouth Harbour, where he could see the famous Red Funnel ferry as it rolled its way over the Solent's gentle swell, heading for the island.

Bazzer was right! Morose could take a trip over to the Isle of Wight, but instead of going there just for a long weekend break, he could take it by force, and claim it as his own! And with an entire island to his name, and with all the resources that would come with it, like running water, and residents who'd probably be trying to do something similar, he could start to build his own private army. And once he'd done that, he could invade Portsmouth and execute Capstan and Bushdew along the way. And if that went according to plan, maybe London? *Why not?* he thought to himself. *It was only just up the M23!*

He turned slowly around to stare, first at Bazzer, and then at Gazzer.

'I think that's just about the best idea I've ever heard in my entire life!'

'Is it?' asked Bazzer, somewhat surprised.

'Definitely!' and he gave them both a demonically-possessed sort of grin.

'Right, men. It's time to get packin', don't you

think?'

Neither Bazzer nor Gazzer knew what to think, given that it wasn't something they'd practised doing very often. So they just nodded as they watched their boss march straight past them, and as soon as Morose was out of earshot, Gazzer turned to Bazzer. 'I've never packed to go on 'oliday before,' he said with childlike excitement. 'What sort of stuff should I take?'

'Nuffin' fancy,' answered Bazzer. 'Just a toothbrush and some bog-roll. They're bound to have loads of shops, so if we need anythin' else, we can just nick it when we get there.'

Chapter Twenty Eight
A journey of some discomfort

Friday, 31ˢᵗ July
04:31 BST

EVEN BEFORE the sun had made an appearance on the horizon, Morose began leading his men out of Portsmouth Prison, which for many had been their permanent residence for more years than they'd care to remember.

As they all started to crunch their way out over the gravel path towards the ten-foot high barbed wire security fence that still encircled them, some four hundred yards away, Bazzer and Gazzer did their best to keep up with their boss, which wasn't easy, as one was carrying an MBT LAW Portable Anti-Tank Guided Missile System, and the other a High Speed StarStreak Anti-Air Missile, both of which were available from the YouGet Arsenal catalogue.

Further hindering their progress was what they were wearing. To help ensure that they blended in with life outside the prison walls, Morose had told them to change out of their comfortable prison overalls and into the clothes that they'd been wearing when they'd arrived, which they'd outgrown at least a decade or two earlier.

But they weren't the only ones. Morose had ordered all the prisoners to change into whatever it was that they'd first arrived in, but due to the length of time most had been locked up for, few clothes fitted properly anymore. They'd either expanded massively or shrunk with old age. So, while some had a real fight to even get into them, others were forced to either punch additional holes in their belts or borrow someone's braces. For most, however, the problem was that of increased girth. Day to day prison life was a sedentary one, which meant that during the process of squeezing themselves back into their pre-prison clothes, a number of inmates had taken a solemn vow not to sit down anywhere, at least not until they'd had a chance to steal something that actually fitted.

Regrettably, this was a problem that Morose hadn't foreseen. If he had, he'd have delayed his planned invasion of the Isle of Wight by a day, so giving everyone a chance to go out shopping. This would have at least made them all look a little more normal, and a little less like they were travelling either to, or from, a week-long Reservoir Dogs Convention.

But it was too late now, and although most of them were walking a bit oddly, which wasn't only because a lot of their trousers were too tight, but also because each had been laden down with some sort of complex piece of advanced military weaponry, at least they didn't look like the mass exodus of escaping prisoners that they actually were.

As more prisoners walked through the main prison gates and onto the gravel path, the noise of escaping prisoners continued to increase, until Morose eventually turned his head to whisper, *'Will everyone please try to walk a little more quietly?'*

The fact that the path leading out to the security fence had been made with gravel, for obvious reasons, was something else that Morose had failed to take into consideration. It had never seemed so bad when he'd walked on it himself, during more sensible daylight hours, but doing so with one hundred and forty-one prisoners behind him at four thirty in the morning was enough to wake the dead, along with the men who'd dug the holes for them.

'Yes, Gov,' whispered Bazzer, and gesticulated around to all those behind him to keep the noise down, forcing them all up onto their tiptoes.

A few minutes later, Gazzer asked, 'Are we nearly there yet?'

He wasn't used to walking on his toes, at least not while carrying an MBT LAW Portable Anti-Tank Guided Missile System. And he certainly wasn't used to having to walk quite such a long way, not in a straight line at any rate. The only exercise he'd been allowed to do for the last thirty years or so had been twice around the prison's main courtyard, but only once each day, and Portsmouth Prison's courtyard really wasn't all that big.

Morose just ignored him.

'Why couldn't we have put all this stuff in the YouGet van, Gov?' asked Bazzer, who was also struggling.

'Because,' answered Morose, 'when I checked the damned thing this morning, it had a flat tyre!'

He was also having to carry an advanced weapons

system, a GX4 Laser Guided Bazooka, but his was relatively light compared to most, although it was digging into his shoulder.

'Why didn't we just change it?' asked Gazzer.

'Because,' answered Morose, 'it had nearly run out of petrol as well. And besides, all this stuff wouldn't have fitted, not with us lot thrown in. No, it's better if we just take the journalists' vans.'

It did make sense, but still didn't change the fact that everyone, apart from Morose, was virtually dead on their feet.

'Are we nearly there yet?' asked Gazzer again.

'For fuck's sake, Gazzer, we've only just left!'

'Sorry, Gov, it's just that I ain't worn these shoes in years, and my feet are killin' me.'

'Tell you what,' said Morose, stopping dead in his tracks and spinning around to stare straight at him. 'If you don't stop moaning, I'll shove this bazooka up your bum and pull the trigger, which, if nothing else, should at least lighten the load!'

'Yes, Gov. Sorry, Gov,' said Gazzer, with the necessary level of subservience, enough at least for Morose to turn back and continue on with the long march towards the security fence.

A few minutes later, Morose reached the gate, and after waiting for everyone else to catch up, asked, 'Right, who's got the keys?'

'I 'ave, Gov,' said Bazzer, as he squeezed his hand into his front trouser pocket in a bid to dig them out.

As the stragglers caught up, they all gathered around Morose, taking much needed time to catch their breath and regain some of their strength. So, before going any further, Morose decided to go over their mission objective, one more time.

'Right men, this is it!' he announced, just loud enough for everyone to hear. 'Once we get through this gate I want you to first incapacitate the journalists—'

A hand shot up from the back.

'Yes, what is it?' came Morose's rather curt response.

'Sorry, Gov, but what does incapacitate mean?'

'Don't *kill* them!' answered Morose. 'They're only journalists after all, and it's probably not their fault. Right! Once they've all been inca— tied up, we need to find the keys to all their trucks and vans. Then we have to ditch all the stuff that's inside them, cameras and whatnot, load up the weapons and climb aboard. Got that?'

Everyone in the crowd nodded.

'Then we're going to drive down to Portsmouth Harbour to catch the Wight Link ferry, which should be leaving at exactly five thirty-five,' he said, glancing down at his watch.

'Why can't we take the Red Funnel ferry instead, Gov?' asked another prisoner, from somewhere in the middle.

'Because Red Funnel only takes pedestrians; not cars, or vans, or trucks,' answered Morose, before moving on. 'The journey across the Solent should take around forty-five minutes, so I suggest we use that time to help ourselves to some breakfast.'

'Do they do a Full English, Gov?' asked someone else.

'I've really no idea,' answered Morose. 'Now, our expected time of arrival at Fishbourne on the Isle of Wight should be around a quarter past six. Once there, we can drive all the vans and trucks off the ferry and make our way up to the Town Hall in Ryde. Then, all we need to do is break in and start letting everyone know that the Isle of Wight is mine— I mean, ours, of course.' He smiled around at his various brothers with armaments. 'Any questions?' he asked magnanimously.

Another hand went up.

'Can I go to the toilet, Gov?'

'No!'

'But I'm desperate, Gov. I think it's these trousers. They're just too tight!'

'Tough shit! You should have gone before we left. You'll just have to wait till we get on the ferry. Anyone else? Yes, you!'

'Won't we need passports, Gov?'

'Obviously not!'

'But I thought they'd become an independent country, Gov?'

'Yes, and? So what?'

'So, won't we need passports to cross the border?'

'No, of course we won't need fucking passports to cross the border!'

'Sorry Gov, but…er, why not?'

Morose let out a heavy sigh.

'Because we've got guns, you dysfunctional, half-brained, moronically inept fuck-wit!'

'Oh,' said the same man, clearly a little disheartened, and in a bid to defend his intelligence, added, 'I just thought they'd need to see something with a photograph on, Gov.'

Morose had momentarily allowed himself to lose his temper, so to help soften his torrent of verbal abuse, said, 'Honestly, I promise, when they see the guns, they won't ask to see any passports. And besides, even if we didn't have guns, I really doubt if anyone would bother to ask.'

He decided that it was probably best not to allow anyone else any more time to think up something else to ask him. 'Right, that's it, men, and as there are no more questions, I suggest we get going.' He nodded at Bazzer.

That was his bodyguard's cue to open the gate, so he stared down at the bunch of keys that somehow he'd managed to wriggle out of his front trouser pocket and began inserting each one into the lock, one at a time, which he thought was probably the quickest, if not the only way, to work out which was the right one.

Chapter Twenty Nine
It simply won't do!

09:29 BST

A S THE LAST few members of Solent's police force, a number of whom were carrying special promotional Safebusy's Forever Bags, on each of which was clearly printed, "Fair Trade Marijuana, HALF PRICE!", shuffled their way into the quieter than normal police briefing room, Chief Inspector Chupples stood behind the lectern at the front with his eyes fixed on the plastic clock on the wall to his left. He was waiting for the short hand to be between the nine and the ten, and the long hand to point directly at the number thirty, which was exactly when the meeting was supposed to start.

Tick-tock, tick-tock, tick-tock, tick!

It was now half-past nine.

'Thank you all for coming,' he announced, glaring at those still finding themselves a seat.

'I don't know if any of you have heard the news, but in the early hours of the morning, the entire population of Portsmouth Prison managed to escape!'

Chupples deliberately paused for effect, expecting to hear an audible gasp rise up from his audience, but he was only met with blank faces, so he continued.

'They were able to do this by incapacitating the

235

dozens of journalists who'd been camping out around the prison.'

He stopped again, half expecting someone to ask what "incapacitating" meant, but nobody did. They all just kept staring at him with their mouths half-open.

'They then had the audacity to steal not just one, but every single van belonging to the TV and news reporters!'

Once more Chupples waited for some sort of demonstrable sign that his audience were as appalled as he was, but none was forthcoming.

'And if that wasn't bad enough,' he continued, 'they then made their way down to the harbour, caught the Wight Link ferry to Fishbourne, disembarked, drove straight up to the Town Hall in Ryde, illegally gained entry to the premises, and announced to the world that they now owned the Isle of Wight!'

Chupples gazed around at his constabulary, desperate for some sort of emotive response to these shameful actions of criminal wrongdoing, but they just kept staring straight back at him, without even blinking, almost as if they'd forgotten how to speak English and subsequently couldn't understand a word he was saying.

'AND IT SIMPLY WON'T DO!' he shouted, bashing his fist on the lectern with some force, in a bid to wake them up out of what seemed to be some sort of trance-like state.

But his audience just followed his fist as it went up and down, and then returned to staring at his face, with the only change to their countenance being that their mouths seemed to be hanging open a little more.

'WHAT IS WRONG WITH YOU PEOPLE?'

A solitary hand was raised by someone sitting in the very first row.

'Yes? You at the front!'

'Is there a buffet?'

Chupples wasn't sure if he'd heard that correctly. 'Sorry, is there a what?'

'A buffet. For breakfast?'

'Is that supposed to be some sort of a joke?'

'I don't think so,' answered the policeman. 'I was just wondering if there was anything to eat, like cornflakes, or maybe some jam on toast.'

'Well, there isn't!'

Another hand went up, from towards the back of the room.

'Yes?'

'If you're looking for someone to tell a joke, Chief Inspector, I know a good one!'

'I don't believe this,' moaned Chupples.

Without waiting for permission to speak, the policeman at the back proceeded to ask everyone around the room, 'What's black and white, and eats like a horse?'

But as nobody seemed to know, he answered it himself.

'A zebra!'

Most of those in attendance involuntarily started to laugh, and began to go a little red as they made a concerted effort not to.

'THE VERY NEXT PERSON WHO TRIES TO BE FUNNY,' bellowed Chupples, as he turned a little puce himself, 'WILL BE FACING A POLICE

DISCIPLINARY TRIBUNAL! IS THAT UNDERSTOOD?'

For the most part, the giggling stopped, and those who were still struggling managed to hide behind the people in front, so at least Chupples couldn't see them.

Regaining his composure, he carried on.

'But unfortunately, as I'm sure you're all aware, the Isle of Wight isn't within our jurisdiction anymore. If it was, then I myself would be over there right now, arresting the lot of them!'

He could still hear at least one person giggling, and narrowed his eyes at everyone around the room. But as he was unable to pinpoint the culprit, he just carried on.

'However, as far as I'm concerned, those responsible are still British Citizens, guilty of crimes committed on British soil. And it is our duty to do all that we can to bring them back here to face justice. With that in mind, I'm looking for two volunteers to head over to the Isle of Wight, undercover, to seek out the main culprits and drag them back here, to Portsmouth, to answer for their actions.'

Dewbush slowly raised a hand, as he used the other to flick back through his notes.'

'Yes, you?'

'Sorry, Chief Inspector, Sir, but what does, "incapacitating" mean?'

'It means tying up, and thank you for being the first to volunteer.'

Unsure as to what he'd just volunteered for, with his hand still in the air he checked back through his notes to see if he'd written it down.

'And you're normally with Inspector Capstan, aren't you? So you can both go!'

In protest, Capstan raised his own hand. 'But Chief Inspector, Sir! I didn't volunteer! And I really don't think Dewbush did either!'

'Well, you both seem to have your hands up, so even if you're not aware of it, you have!'

Bringing his hand back down, Capstan muttered, *'Unbelievable,'* under his breath.

'You can take a motor launch from the harbour,' continued Chupples. 'The Duty Officer has the keys, and I expect a full report, if not the miscreants themselves, back here by end of play today!'

Chapter Thirty
Of milk and men

11:07 BST

AS CLAIRE MADE herself comfortable in the extra chair that had been provided for her to attend this, her second Cabinet Meeting, her uncle stood up to address his assembled Ministers.

'Before we start, I'd firstly like to re-introduce my niece, who's here purely in an advisory capacity. Frankly, without her having been around recently, I'd have probably been assassinated by now, so although it is against tradition, I'm going to have to insist that she stays.'

He glared around the room at everyone, almost daring any of them to make some sort of a derogatory remark, or to lodge an official complaint, but his Cabinet all nodded almost in unison and smiled at her. For even though she didn't belong there, and despite the fact that they were all jealous of the complimentary remarks she'd received, which few of them had ever been on the receiving end of, she remained as easy-on-the-eye as ever and were delighted to have another opportunity to letch.

'And secondly, I'd like to state for the record that I'm becoming increasingly miffed at having to show my face at another one of these so-called Emergency

Meetings.'

As the Home Secretary, Harold Percy-Blakemore, had been the one to call for it, he leaned forward in his chair positioned to Robert's immediate right and said, 'Yes, of course, Prime Minister.'

'Especially when I'm not the one who asked to hold one!'

'Absolutely, Prime Minister,' agreed Harold again.

'And if this one isn't a real emergency, and by that I mean that some deranged psychotic terrorist hasn't escaped from an MI6 holding cell and is, at this precise moment in time, down in the car park waiting to detonate a nuclear warhead from inside the boot of my Range Rover, then frankly, I doubt if I'm going to be interested.'

'I fully understand, Prime Minister,' said Harold again, doing a remarkable job at expressing empathy, 'but I really do feel that this *is* an emergency situation, and one that needs the whole Cabinet's most urgent attention.'

'Well, it better be!'

'I'm extremely sure that it is, Prime Minister.'

'Get on with it then. Unlike you, I haven't got all bloody day.' Robert glowered down at Harold who was deliberately avoiding eye contact, before re-taking his seat.

With a quick inhalation, the Home Secretary stood up and started his pre-planned and well-rehearsed speech.

'Thank you, Prime Minister. At exactly seven twenty-eight this morning, I received a telephone call from Florence Ruddy-Shelduck, the Chairperson for the People's Independent Republic of the Isle of Wight.'

He then took a conscious moment to engage eye contact with all those sitting around the table, and when he reached the Prime Minister, Robert asked, 'Was that it?'

'Er, not quite, Prime Minister.'

'Are you sure?' asked Robert again.

'I'm pretty sure, Prime Minister.'

'It's just that it sounded like you'd finished.'

Being careful not to publicly contradict his Prime Minister, Harold said, 'I don't think so, Prime Minister,' and before Robert could interrupt him for a second time, decided to give up with the clever use of dramatic pauses and pushed on with what he'd planned to say, just as quickly as possible.

'In the early hours of this morning, a heavily armed force landed at Fishbourne, a small coastal village on the Isle of Wight. From there they drove straight up to the Town Hall in Ryde, illegally gained entry, and shortly afterwards, announced to the world that they'd taken control of the island.'

'Do they have any nuclear weapons?' asked Robert.

'We're not sure, at this stage, Prime Minister.'

'So, therefore, is it safe for us to assume that one of them hasn't just driven into the car park underneath the building, and is currently in the process of unloading a weapon of mass destruction into the boot of my car in preparation for triggering a thirty second countdown timer?'

'It's probably unlikely, Prime Minister.'

'Then it isn't an emergency, is it?' stated Robert,

sneering with disdain at his Home Secretary.

'I think that could depend on one's definition of the word *emergency*, Prime Minister.'

'Is that so? And what, may I ask, is your definition of the word, *emergency*?'

'Well, Prime Minister,' began Harold, as he pulled his collar away from his neck, 'without being able to look it up in the Oxford English Dictionary, I'd say that it's defined as being a, er, situation that threatens the lives of large numbers of people.'

'That sounds about right,' agreed Robert, and was amused to see Harold's face brighten with relief. 'But, unfortunately, you missed out a word that I'd consider to be fundamentally necessary to substantiate your argument.'

'I did, Prime Minister?'

'You did, Harold. Now, can anyone guess what that word might be?'

It was Robert's turn to gaze around at all those in attendance, with the exception of Claire.

Gerald Frackenburger, the Defence Minister, slowly raised his hand.

'Yes, Gerald?'

'Did he forget to say, Prime Minister, Prime Minister?'

'I think he did, Gerald, but that's not what I was thinking of. Anyone else?'

But nobody seemed to know, and if they did, they certainly weren't prepared to volunteer an answer.

'British!' exclaimed Robert. 'The word he missed out was "British!" And the last time I looked, the Isle of Wight wasn't!'

'Well, no, Prime Minister, but…'

'And may I add that their all-too recent vote to become independent from the United Kingdom was their choice, Harold. Their choice! Not ours!'

'Of course, Prime Minister, but they *are* still a member of the Commonwealth. And as they're a small island,' continued Harold, in their defence, 'just a few miles off our coast, it feels only right to discuss the idea of offering them our assistance, Prime Minister.'

'As is often the case, Harold, you've completely missed the point.'

'I have, Prime Minister?'

Robert gave Harold a magnanimous smile.

'Indeed, you have, Harold.'

But Harold looked none the wiser, so Robert continued.

'I'm not suggesting that we don't discuss the fact that they've been taken over by a hostile armed force. I'm questioning your decision to classify it as an emergency - one that could have a potential impact on the lives of large numbers of British citizens - and so forcing me into the same room as you lot for no bloody good reason!'

'Er, yes, Prime Minister.'

'I think we see quite enough of each other already, don't you?'

'Of course, Prime Minister, I-I mean, not at all, Prime Minister.'

'So anyway, I suggest that next time you think an emergency situation has arisen, you let *me* decide if it is one or not. Is that understood, Harold?'

'Fully, Prime Minister,' and he bowed his head with

the correct level of submissive humble servitude.

'OK, good. So anyway, now that we're all here, you'd better get on with it.'

Privately, Robert didn't mind too much. The evening before, he'd sampled some of the Isle of Wight's produce, and for the very first time, which had been followed moments later by the best sex he'd ever had in his entire life. He was subsequently keen to ensure that the island was able to keep up with its supply of their most extraordinary little cash crop, and it didn't sound like an armed hostile invasion would help much.

'Yes, Prime Minister. In the early hours of...'

'You've just said all that!'

'Sorry, Prime Minister. So, to cut to the chase, as it were, I'd like to propose that we send over a special Task Force, just as soon as the constraints of time will allow, to re-take the island and place it back into the hands of those to whom it rightfully belongs.'

'You mean us?' asked Robert.

'Er, no, Prime Minister. I meant the People's Independent Republic of the Isle of Wight, Prime Minister.'

'And by Task Force, I assume you're referring to something like the one we sent over to the Falklands?'

'That's correct, Prime Minister.'

'With giant-sized battleships, hulking great aircraft carriers, Harrier Jump Jet things and Sidewinder missiles?'

'Correct again, Prime Minister.'

There was a momentary pause, after which Robert asked, 'Have you completely lost your mind?'

'Er, not at all, Prime Minister. I'm simply putting forward a suggestion that has been historically proven to be highly successful in re-taking a small island, Prime Minister.'

'Yes, but the Falkland Islands were miles away!'

Robert wasn't sure how many miles away they were, exactly, but was confident, at least, that it was more than one.

'I think you'll find that they still are, Prime Minister,' muttered Harold, unable to say it without a heavy sarcastic undertone. But he was certainly chancing his arm, along with all his other appendages.

Fortunately for him, Robert decided to ignore it. 'And the Isle of Wight is…well, Harold, it's just over there!' and pointed in the vague sort of direction of where he thought it should be. 'In fact,' he added, 'we can probably see it from here,' and was about to suggest that they all head up to his office to have a look through his new telescope, when Harold interrupted his chain of thought.

'That may be so, Prime Minister, but we'd still need to send out an armed force over a stretch of water in order eject the insurgents, which certainly is a remarkably similar scenario to the Falklands, Prime Minister.'

'But surely we could send over something smaller, and considerably less expensive?'

'May I ask what you would propose instead, Prime Minister?'

'I've no idea, Harold, but probably something more like a fishing boat, or a dinghy. Even a bloody milk-float would probably do the trick!'

'I'm sorry, Prime Minister, but I don't think milk floats actually…er, float, Prime Minister.'

'Really, Harold. I'd no idea!'

'Unfortunately not, Prime Minister. Milk floats are effectively vans that are used primarily to deliver dairy produce, like milk, for example. They're also battery-operated which, although it makes them very quiet, and so less likely to wake people up when they make their early morning rounds, does make them rather heavy, Prime Minister.'

Robert couldn't quite believe what he was having to listen to, but it at least proved one thing; his Home Secretary probably started his working life as a milkman, which explained a lot. And as his eyes darted around at the various objects scattered around the opaque glass boardroom table, hoping to find something both heavy and sharp enough to put a sizable dent in Harold's head, Gerald Frackenburger raised his hand once more.

Unable to find anything other than a Bic biro, but still furtively looking, Robert glanced up at him.

'Yes, Gerald?'

'I may have an alternative solution, Prime Minister.'

'I think anything anyone else has to offer must have more validity than that of our synoptically-challenged Home Secretary sitting before us here, so please, Gerald, do carry on.'

'It may be that we could have a chat with the Royal Marines, Prime Minister. A military assault on the Island would necessitate the use of both the land and the sea, and they did do a commendable job when re-taking the Falklands. And if we were able to use them, it would rule out the need for either the Royal Navy or the Air Force, Prime Minister.'

'It's good to see that someone here has at least managed to maintain some functionality of their brain. Well done, Gerald! Can you try to get hold of them now?'

'Of course, Prime Minister.' He reached over to pull forward the conference phone system that lay in the centre of the table, alongside a jug of mineral water.

A few moments later he announced, 'I have the Royal Marines Commandant General, Major General John Draycote for you, Prime Minister.'

'Could you just put him on speaker phone for me?'

'Yes, Prime Minister,' and after pressing the relevant button, he announced, 'Major General, I have the Prime Minister for you.'

'Good morning, Prime Minister,' came the clipped voice of the Royal Marines Commandant General from the speaker phone system.

Before answering, Robert whispered over to Gerald, *'What was his name again?'*

'John; John Draycote, Prime Minister.'

'Hello, John, and how are you today?' asked Robert, with his voice raised loud enough to carry over to the phone.

'Very well, thank you, Prime Minister.'

'That's good to hear. Now John, we have a situation here that we need to talk to you about. It's not an *emergency* situation, by any means,' stated Robert, narrowing his eyes at his Home Secretary, 'but probably more of a…quandary situation, so to speak.'

'I'm more than happy to be of service in any way I can, Prime Minister.'

'There's a good chap. May I first ask if you've heard of the Isle of Wight?'

'Yes, I believe I have, Prime Minister.'

'Excellent! And have you been made aware of the fact that it was taken over by an armed force this morning.'

'It has been featured on the news, yes, Prime Minister.'

'Great! And how would you feel about heading over there with some of your men to re-take it?'

'In theory, Prime Minister, I'd have to say that it would be an acceptable mission for us, but would probably depend on the timescales that you had in mind.'

'Do you mean; how long we think it would take for you to re-gain control of the island?' asked Robert, a little confused.

'Er, no, Prime Minister. More of when you wanted us to head over there.'

'I see,' said Robert, who was of the understanding that the British Armed Forces were supposed to be at his instant and immediate beck and call, and with an air of irritation, asked, 'Are you particularly busy at the moment, Major General?'

'Unfortunately not, Prime Minister, but we do seem to be having a few, how can I put it, a few morale issues, at the moment, Prime Minister.'

'Morale issues?'

'I think that would be the correct term, yes, Prime Minister.'

'Caused by what, may I ask?'

'Safebusy's half-price sale of Fair Trade Marijuana, Prime Minister.'

'And how on earth has a Safebusy's sale had a demotivational impact?'

'It's not so much the sale itself, Prime Minister, but more the widespread consumption by my men of what was, until just last week, a banned narcotic substance. And it seems to have taken away their interest in anything other than eating sweet baked products, and, er, partaking in carnal pleasures, Prime Minister.'

'I see,' said Robert, with rare and unusual insight.

'And we're just trying to work out what we can do about it, Prime Minister.'

'Can't you just tell them to stop smoking it?'

'Well, Prime Minister, we have ordered them to, of course, but it's proving difficult to detect when half them already smoke traditional cigarettes. So instead, we're exploring ways to re-motivate them, Prime Minister.'

'I'd have thought that asking a soldier to re-take the Isle of Wight would have been motivation enough!'

'If it was still a part of the British Isles, then it probably would have been, yes, Prime Minister.'

'I see your point,' said Robert.

'What we need,' continued the Commandant General, *'is something to help counteract the effects of the marijuana, and that would also give them the impetus to fight, Prime Minister.'*

Robert saw a hand go up from out of the corner of his eye.

It was Claire.

'Yes, my dear, you have an idea?'

'I was just thinking about what some of my University friends used to do to help offset the lethargic effects of smoking marijuana,' said Claire.

'And what was that?' asked Robert.

'Well, this wasn't me, of course, but whenever they had to finish off an assignment, or study for an exam, or go to an all-night party, they used to take cocaine.'

'Cocaine?' asked Robert, beginning to wonder what Claire had really been getting up to at University.

'That's right. And it always seemed to do the trick.'

'Right then,' said Robert, as his mind processed the idea that his niece was an avid cocaine user. 'Does anyone here know where we can get hold of a decent amount of cocaine?'

Harold raised his hand.

'This better be good,' said Robert.

And in a bid to win back a few brownie points, Harold said, 'We actually seized a large amount of what we suspect is cocaine last night, after a daring car chase down the M23. And it's now being held by MI6, at their headquarters in Vauxhall.'

'I think we have our answer then,' said Robert, with a winning smile. 'I'd therefore like to propose that we send Claire here, along with the cocaine, straight over to our Royal Marine chums, the combination of which I'd have thought would be enough to re-invigorate a comatose rhino. Are we all in agreement?'

And as nobody said they weren't, Robert called to the Royal Marines Commandant General, who was still listening in from the other end of the phone, 'John, I'm going to send my niece, Claire Bridlestock, over to you, along with a shipment of cocaine. It's up to you what you do with it, but Claire seems to think that it may be a good pick-me-up for your men. And then, if you could pop yourselves over to the Isle of Wight, that would be most appreciated.'

'Yes, of course, Prime Minister.'

Robert gesticulated to Gerald to end the call, and then grinned, first at Claire, and then at everyone else in the room, before asking, 'Can I go now?'

Chapter Thirty One
An obligation of duty

12:51 BST

'IT'S JUST LIKE old times, isn't it, Sir?' said Dewbush, as they chugged and spluttered their way out in a beaten-up old motor launch, across a Solent that twinkled in the bright early afternoon sun of yet another glorious British summer's day.

'Is it?' asked Capstan, staring through a pair of police issue binoculars at what seemed to be an endless number of white sailing-type boat things, all of which he was keen to avoid.

'You know, Sir. Like the time we had to chase after HMS Victory, Sir.'

'Just keep your eyes peeled, Dewbush. There are far more boats out here now than there were back then, and none of them seem to have a clue where they're going.'

'They do seem to keep changing direction rather a lot, Sir,' he agreed as they both watched a particularly large one tack over onto starboard and begin heading straight for them.

'I think they have right of way,' said Capstan, who'd removed his binoculars to stare at the approaching vessel.

'How'd you mean, Sir?'

'I mean, Dewbush, that we have to keep clear.'

'Right you are, Sir.' Dewbush turned the boat over to port in a bid to avoid them. As he did so, the glistening white yacht began to tack over again, so they ended up set back on a collision course.

'You need to turn it the other way, Dewbush,' advised Capstan.

'If you say so, Sir.'

Dewbush started to turn the boat once more, this time over to starboard. The yacht began to do the same; and so it wasn't long before they were, once again, heading straight at each other, and edging ever closer with each passing moment.

'I think they're deliberately trying to ram us, Sir,' suggested Dewbush.

'I doubt it.'

'You know, Sir, it could be that they're insurgents, from the Isle of Wight, Sir.'

'Is that so, Dewbush?'

'They may have heard that we were coming, and sent out some of their men to stop us, Sir.'

'Really, Dewbush?'

'They may even be mercenaries, Sir, which must mean that there's a price on our heads!'

'The only price that could ever be on your head, Dewbush, would be 99p, and that would only attract the sort of hired assassin who'd be more likely to shoot themselves before managing to kill anyone else.'

'Yes, Sir. But it's possible though, Sir, isn't it?'

'Well, I suppose, Dewbush. However, just as likely is that they're a ship-load of mutated mice who, having completed their RYA Day Skipper's Course, have set sail to take over the world, one boat at a time.'

'Personally, Sir, I think that's far less likely.'

'You could be right, Dewbush, but as we're about to plough straight into that yacht, I'd strongly recommend that you stick this thing into reverse!'

'Right you are, Sir.'

As they edged their way backwards, so avoiding what was to be only one of many near-misses that day, Capstan and Dewbush continued to pick their way through the myriad of sailing vessels as the People's Republic of the Isle of Wight grew ever larger.

About an hour later, what had seemed like a mysterious distant land now looked much like any other, and they began to search for somewhere suitable to moor up.

'Shouldn't we just head for one of the harbours, Sir?' asked Dewbush, steering the motor launch parallel with the coastline as Capstan peered out over the side.

'It's probably better if we don't, Dewbush. We're supposed to be working undercover, and I'd prefer it if we didn't attract any unnecessary attention.'

'Look, Sir! There's a man, and he's waving some sort of a weapon at us!'

'Yes, I can see,' said Capstan, as he lifted his binoculars to his eyes again to focus in on him.

'Is it a machine gun, Sir?'

'It looks more like a rake, but he is wearing some sort of military-style khaki bandana around his head.'

'Shall I wave back, Sir?'

'It's probably better if you don't, Dewbush. Not

until we know whose side he's on.'

'How about I show him my ID, Sir? Just so that he knows we're from the police.'

'As we're still supposed to be undercover, Dewbush, that's probably not one of your best ideas. And anyway, I doubt if he'd be able to see it from all the way over there.'

'I suppose not, Sir.'

'Look, there's a stretch of beach,' said Capstan, pointing to near where the man was still waving a rake at them. 'I suggest you try to land there. Hopefully we'll then be able to have a chat with him and at least find out if he's friend or foe. And if he's on our side, he should be able to point us in the direction of the insurgents.'

'And if he's not, Sir?'

'Then we'll just have to pretend that we're lost, and ask him for directions back to England.'

'Okay, Sir. I'll have a go at a landing.' Dewbush turned the wheel around and began heading towards the sandy area that Capstan had been referring to.

Once Dewbush had nudged the nose of the motor launch up onto the beach, he and Capstan cautiously made their way along the boat's sides towards the bow, where Dewbush was able to jump onto the sand, before turning to help his boss. The man they'd observed earlier scrambled down an escarpment of rocks as if to intercept them.

'Are you the police?' he called, as he made his way over.

Somewhat put out to have had their cover blown quite so quickly, Capstan asked, 'What on earth makes you think that?'

'Er, because it's written in large capital letters all the way down the side of your boat.'

Capstan and Dewbush turned to stare at their motor launch. They'd become so used to driving around in an unmarked police car, they'd completely forgotten about the boat's rather obvious signage.

'We could have stolen it,' stated Dewbush, in a rather sad effort to remain undercover.

But the man with the garden rake only frowned at him.

'Okay, we're the police,' admitted Capstan, and flashed his formal identification. 'I'm Inspector Capstan and this is Sergeant Dewbush. We're from the Solent Constabulary. And who might you be?'

'My name's Giles Partisan. I'm the Secretary of Agriculture for the People's Independent Republic of the Isle of Wight.'

'I see,' said Capstan, eyeing the man's rake that still looked a little menacing.

'At least I was,' continued the man with a forlorn, wistful expression. 'But now I'm a member of what we're calling The People's Independent Republic of the Isle of Wight's Resistance Movement.'

'Isn't that a bit of a mouthful?' asked Capstan.

'Not really.'

Capstan shrugged, and then thought to ask, 'And why were you waving that rake at us just now?'

'I was trying to attract your attention. We've been taken over, you see, by hundreds of men, all armed with advanced military weaponry, and we desperately need some help!'

'Hundreds of them, did you say?' asked Capstan, scanning the rocks and shrubs for any sign of hostile movement.

'Well, we haven't had a chance to count them all, yet, but I'd have to say that there were certainly quite a few.'

'And all armed with advanced military weapons?'

'That's right. Missile launchers, bazookas, that sort of thing.'

'I see,' said Capstan, trying to decide if that was enough information to justify their immediate departure back to base, where they could write up their report from what must have been a much safer distance from where they were currently standing.

'I'd better take you to meet our Chairperson,' said Giles, and he turned to begin leading them away from what felt like the relative safety of the beach.

'Um,' called out Capstan, after him.

But the man had already reached the base of the escarpment and probably couldn't hear him.

'Shall we go with him, Sir?' asked Dewbush, who'd clearly become as concerned for his personal welfare as Capstan had. But as much as Capstan would have liked to have told the man that they'd better be on their way, before wishing him and his resistance movement the very best of luck, he felt he'd already missed the opportunity.

'C'mon, Dewbush. We'd better at least meet the rest of them. And hopefully that will give us enough time to think of a good enough reason to head back to Portsmouth and let them get on with it without us.'

Chapter Thirty Two
Stage presence

13:17 BST

WITH A LARGE black holdall stuffed full of cocaine, and her favourite Gucci handbag, Claire stepped out of her uncle's private helicopter onto the airfield located at a small village called Bickleigh, just eight miles north east of Plymouth in Devon, the home to the 56 Royal Marines Commando Unit.

There to meet her was a lean, middle-aged soldier with a weathered, tanned face and striking good looks. Giving Claire a karate-chop sort of a salute that could easily have taken out a knife-wielding assassin, maybe even two, he said, 'Welcome to Bickleigh Barracks. I'm Lieutenant Colonel Frank Derwent and I'm the Commanding Officer here.'

'Oh, hello!' said Claire, feeling unusually bashful, 'My name's Claire Bridlestock. I'm the Prime Minister's Marketing and Public Relations Consultant.'

'So I've heard,' said the Lieutenant Colonel, and as they exchanged smiles the Commanding Officer continued, 'Would you like some help with that bag?'

'If you could, that would be great,' she said, adding, 'Thank you, Lieutenant Colonel,' for good measure.

'My pleasure, and please, call me Frank.' He smiled

259

again, lifting up the holdall with one hand and heaving it up onto his shoulder.

'Now, I understand that this almost qualifies as being an emergency situation, so I've taken the liberty of having the men assembled in the mess hall, ready for your briefing.'

'My briefing?' asked Claire, with some alarm.

'Yes, you know, to chat to them about the mission and to see if you can jolly them up a bit.'

'Oh, right, of course. It's just that I was only expecting to be discussing the idea with you.'

'Well, I'll be there, so in effect you will be. If you just follow me, I'll take you through,' and he pivoted around on one foot and began to march off towards a red brick building set on the edge of the tarmac airfield.

'Right,' said Claire to herself. 'Fair enough,' and girding her loins, along with her handbag, set off at a fair pace in an effort to catch him up. But that was far from easy, given her three-inch high Gianvito Rossi cream-coloured stilettoes that she'd only bought the week before; but despite having found herself lugging a huge black holdall from MI6 Headquarters opposite Vauxhall Bridge, all the way down to Devon via the combination of a chauffeur-driven Land Rover Discovery and a Liquidator Super X-6000 helicopter, she was still pleased she'd chosen to wear them that morning as they went perfectly with yet another of her near-transparent summer dresses, this one featuring a plunging neckline and a hem that barely covered her thighs. And with her general dislike for having to wear bras, especially during the warm summer months, once again she looked to the untrained eye to be completely naked.

The Lieutenant Colonel had stopped beside the entrance, and as she clicked and bounced her way over the tarmac towards him, he pulled the door open and held it as he took a moment to enjoy watching her.

'Thank you,' she said, a little out of breath.

'The pleasure was all mine,' he said, with a smile that could have charmed her pants off, had she been wearing any. But for Claire, pants fell into the same category as bras during the summer; and given her current location, "going commando" seemed strangely appropriate.

Inside the entrance hall stood four more Royal Marines who, on seeing their Commanding Officer, plus guest, stood to attention and raised their right hands in unison to their foreheads with such alacrity that it looked as if it was a deliberate attempt to give themselves a concerted chop, possibly in a bid to demonstrate their above average tolerance to pain.

Maintaining a steady salute, two of them pulled open the double glass doors to Claire's left, and held them wide.

'Well done, men,' said Lieutenant Colonel Frank Derwent to the two in charge of the doors, who, having been able to open them with such military precision, must have been specially trained.

'Everyone's through here,' he told Claire, and stepped into what looked like the back of a school assembly hall, but which, instead of children, was packed full of similar-sized shaven-headed young men wearing identical khaki uniforms, all quietly talking amongst themselves.

Claire hesitated; but as the Lieutenant Colonel was already half-way down the hall, marching his way between what must have been hundreds of Royal Marine Commandos, heading for a stage at the far end on which stood a solitary lectern, she thought it best to clatter and bounce her way down the highly polished wooded floor after him.

As she did so, the hundreds of shorn heads ended their various conversations and began turning around to look at who it was with the stilettoes that they could so clearly hear. And with all talk now ended, the only sound left to echo around the hall was Claire in her Gianvito Rossi's.

At the base of the stage the Lieutenant Colonel stopped and turned to wait for her again. He ushered her up onto the raised platform and made his way over to the lectern in order to address his men.

'Good afternoon! I'm sure you're all wondering why you've been gathered here today. I have with me the Prime Minister's very own Marketing and Public Relations Consultant, Miss Claire Bridlestock, who's flown all the way from Number 10 Downing Street in Canary Wharf, to be with us, in order to give you an idea as to what our next assignment is going to be.'

He then stood to one side and offered Claire his place.

With a gulp, she stepped forward and took her position behind the lectern.

As she did so, the two hundred or so men on her right-hand side all leaned away from the centre of the hall, just as all those on the left did the opposite, every one of them attempting to peer around the annoying wooden object that was obscuring their view of this unimaginably gorgeous young lady, who must work as a Page 3 model in her spare time and, judging by her choice of clothes, must have been on her way to her next photoshoot.

Clearing her throat, Claire attempted to catch the eyes of at least one of the hundreds of men, but they all seemed to be intent on trying to stare at the rest of her, so she thought she'd better just get on with it.

'Hello, my name's Claire Bridlestock,' she said, with as much confidence as she could muster. 'As your, er, the, um, Lieutenant Colonel here has just said, I'm the Prime Minister's Marketing and Public Relations Consultant.'

She paused, not for dramatic effect, but more to make sure that everyone could hear her, as not a single one of them had moved so much as a muscle since she'd taken her place behind the lectern. And the only sound she could hear was that of her heart pounding deep within her heaving bosom. So she decided to just carry on regardless of whether they could hear her or not, and taking a leaf out of her uncle's book, started by asking them, 'Has anyone here heard of the Isle of Wight?'

But nobody so much as raised an eyebrow, let alone a hand, so to help clarify her question she added, 'It's actually now called The People's Republic of the Isle of Wight.' But it made no difference; the four hundred or so Royal Marines continued to do their best to ogle her from around the lectern.

'Anyway,' she continued, 'it's a small island off the

South Coast of England that was, until recently, part of the United Kingdom, but has since become an independent country.'

Sill not a sound, shuffle, word or comment came from the assembled men, and she glanced behind her to make sure that at least Frank was still there. He sent her an encouraging smile.

So she turned back to face the 56 Royal Marines Commando Unit, and pushed on.

'In the early hours of this morning, a heavily armed group of insurgents landed on the island, made their way up to the Town Hall in Ryde, forced their way into the building and declared ownership. Now although, as I mentioned earlier, the People's Republic of the Isle of Wight isn't a part of the United Kingdom anymore, they are still very much a part of the Commonwealth, and as such it's being asked of you to re-take the island with a view to handing it back to those to whom it rightfully belongs.'

A single hand went up from the third row, and with relief that at least someone had been listening, Claire asked, 'Yes?'

'Is that us?'

'Er, no,' she answered, 'unfortunately it would still need to be handed back to the People's Republic of the Isle of Wight.'

'I meant, is it *us* you want to go over there to re-take it?'

'Oh, sorry! My fault,' she said. 'I didn't make it clear. Yes, we'd like you, the 56 Royal Marines Commando Unit, to go over there and re-take control.'

Feeling as if she'd at last begun to make progress,

she continued, 'And by way of thanks, we have some goodie-bags for you.' She turned to their Commanding Officer to say quietly, 'Could you possibly ask someone to pass around the samples from inside the holdall?'

During the last few minutes Frank had become mesmerized by her near-perfect, and almost naked bum of which, unlike everyone else in the hall, he'd had a clear and unobstructed view. Caught in the act, he jumped, saying, 'Oh! Yes, of course, sorry,' and with a sheepish smile, carried the holdall that he'd completely forgotten was still over his shoulder to the edge of the stage. He heaved it off and unzipped its top to reveal hundreds of small clear plastic bags, each crammed full of white powder. He crouched and passed the holdall down to the nearest soldier, saying, 'You men on the front row; hand these sample bags out, one to every person.'

He stood up again and returned to his place just behind Claire, keeping a close eye on his men to make sure they carried out his order to the letter.

The soldier sitting on the third row received his bag, turned it over a few times, and raised his hand.

Claire pointed at him. 'Yes, you again?'

'What's in the bag, Miss?'

'Good question,' she answered, and as it was one that she and the Cabinet had been expecting, and as they were all keen not to make it public knowledge that they intended to hand out an illegal "A" class drug to an entire Royal Marines Commando Unit, she said exactly what she'd been told to.

'It's a completely safe, all-natural, state-of-the-art,

tried-and-tested, brand new performance-enhancing drug that's just arrived from America.'

'What's it called?' asked the same soldier.

'Um,' answered Claire. Unfortunately that wasn't a question she, or anyone else, had been expecting; but thinking fast on her feet, which she was good at, she delved into her vast knowledge of the cosmetics industry and came up with, 'Cocainebelieve,' and was going to add, *'because you're w——!'* but changed her mind at the last minute.

'And how do we take it, Miss?'

'You can use it as a sugar substitute by sprinkling it on your Corn Flakes, or you can rub it into your gums. But I've been advised that the very best method of ingestion is to, er, snort it, up your nose, just before engaging with the enemy.'

Another soldier raised his hand, this time from the middle left, and without waiting for permission to speak, asked, 'Will you be coming with us, Miss?'

'I'm sorry, but to where?' she asked.

'To the People's Independent Republic of the Isle of Wight, Miss.'

'Who, me?' she answered, clearly shocked at the very suggestion.

'Yes, you, Miss?'

'Well-I-I-er-um…' she spluttered, as she desperately tried to think of some sort of valid reason why, under absolutely no circumstances, was she able to go anywhere near the island, not while it was still under the control of heavily armed insurgents, and certainly not when another armed force was about to be sent in to begin a hostile military engagement with them.

'I think we'd all really appreciate it if you could, Miss.'

'You could accompany the Rear Command Unit,' offered Lieutenant Colonel Frank Derwent, as a more practical alternative. 'You'd be perfectly safe from there, and I'm sure that we'd all appreciate knowing that you were willing us on from behind.'

And as she gazed into his tanned, rugged features, and the steel-blue eyes, all the possible horrors of war were forgotten, and with an almost indiscernible blush, and the merest flicker of her heavily mascaraed eyelashes, said, 'I'd be delighted to, Frank, and thank you for asking!'

Chapter Thirty Three
A complimentary remark

13:38 BST

HAVING SPENT the best part of an hour traipsing through dense deciduous island undergrowth, Giles Partisan, the Secretary of Agriculture for the People's Independent Republic of the Isle of Wight's Resistance Movement, finally led Inspector Capstan and Sergeant Dewbush out into a clearing.

Ahead was a small campfire, surrounded by a dozen or so people, all wearing the same green wellies and bandanas that must have been a part of the island's traditional dress. Immediately before them stood two giant men carrying sharpened shovels and wearing the same matching wellies and head scarfs, who together formed an impenetrable barrier, and they were glaring directly at Capstan and Dewbush with clear, malicious intent.

Seeing the look in their eyes, and the glint of their gardening tools, Giles said quickly, 'Don't worry, comrades, they're with me,' and with a low grunt of approval, the tree-trunk like men stepped to one side to let the approaching party pass.

Those gathered around the fire all turned to see who the strangers were.

268

'Who've you got there, Giles?' asked a plump, middle aged woman with a mess of grey hair that was being kept under control by her ubiquitous khaki bandana.

'Two policeman, from the United Kingdom, Comrade. I found them on the beach, down in Osborne Bay.'

'And what do they want?'

'They've come about the insurgents, Comrade.'

'That's good!' said the woman. 'I don't suppose there's any more of them?' she asked, as she stared over at the one she assumed to be the senior, because he looked older, and had a stick.

'It's just us, I'm afraid,' answered Capstan, struggling for breath as he limped his way towards the group. His gammy leg was in agony, and because of it he was exhausted. It was rare for him to have to walk anywhere back in Portsmouth, and certainly not through dense deciduous undergrowth.

Standing up from the log on which she'd been sitting, the grey-haired woman said, 'I'm sorry, but we'd better see some sort of identification before you come any closer.'

'Oh, of course,' said Capstan, and used that as an excuse to rest for a moment as he removed his formal police ID from inside his suit jacket pocket. 'I'm Inspector Capstan and this is my colleague, Sergeant Dewbush,' and as he held his badge out at arms-length for her to see, added, 'We're from Solent Police.'

'I see,' said the woman, 'but you know that you don't have jurisdiction here anymore, don't you?'

'Yes, ma'am. We've been made aware of that.'

'Please, not *ma'am*. My name's Florence Ruddy-Shelduck. I'm the Chairperson of the People's Independent Republic of the Isle of Wight's Resistance Movement.' She bounded over to him with her hand extended like a happy-go-lucky sheep dog performing a well-rehearsed trick.

With a firm shake, Capstan said, 'It's a pleasure to meet you, Chairperson Florence.'

'Call me Flo,' she said, and gave him a toothy grin. She lolloped over to Sergeant Dewbush to extend the same welcome.

'So, what exactly are you doing here?'

'We've been sent over to do a little reconnaissance, really,' answered Capstan, deciding not to divulge that their given objective had actually been to re-arrest the invading insurgents before escorting them back to Portsmouth Prison, just in case their new adversaries waved them off in the right direction with an encouraging slap on the back. 'But we're pretty much done now,' he added, 'so we'd better be off.'

'That's a shame,' said Florence, 'and we've only just put the kettle on. Wouldn't either of you like a nice cup of tea before you go?'

'I would!' said Dewbush, raising his hand as he was prone to.

Capstan was also desperately parched, and as keen as he was to get back to the relative safety of their boat, knowing that they'd have another hour long trek back through half the island's undergrowth, said, 'If it's not too much trouble, that would be nice, thank you.'

'Two more teas please, Comrade Brian,' said Florence, as she offered Capstan and Dewbush a log each to sit on.

'As you're here,' she said, in a conversational tone, 'maybe you could help us think up some ideas to get our island back.'

Capstan eased himself down onto the tree stump with a liberating groan, and looked around at the eclectic mix of people who all gazed back at him with an air of hopeless expectation. Judging by the look of them, they'd have been more at home fending off an invasion of herbivorous slugs than a heavily armed force of dangerous criminals.

'What have you come up with so far?' he asked, out of idle curiosity.

'Not much. Comrade Jeffrey here suggested we sign a petition, asking them to make a peaceful withdrawal. Comrade James thought it would be better if we went over to the Town Hall in person, under a white flag of truce, and ask if they wouldn't mind leaving, and our very own Comrade John Long-Silverton here suggested an all-out attack! But at the moment we're thinking of a combination of the first two; to draw up a petition and hand-deliver it, at which point we could ask them if they wouldn't mind being on their way.'

'They all sound really good,' said Capstan, with unusual diplomacy, 'but before you do that, maybe you could have a go at weakening their resolve a little?'

'How'd you mean?' asked Florence.

'You know; make life difficult for them by blowing up a bridge, or something. It's what the French Resistance did during World War Two.'

'I see,' said Flo, 'but I'm not sure that we've got any bridges.'

'How about a train?' asked Capstan.

'You'd better ask our Secretary of Vehicles and Recreation.' Looking over at an emaciated middle-aged man sitting opposite with sunken cheeks and a permanent frown, she asked, 'Comrade Brian, do we have any trains?'

Hearing his name he sat up with a start. 'Oh, er, yes,' he said. 'We certainly do! There's a regular service running from Ryde Pierhead that connects the east and south of the island. And we've also got a fully operational steam one, but that's more for the tourists, and I doubt we'll be getting many of those anymore.'

'Well, if you blew up all the railway lines,' said Capstan, 'that would probably be enough to cause a fair amount of disruption.'

'Right,' said Comrade Flo, and with renewed resolve, asked, 'I don't suppose anyone knows if we have any dynamite knocking about?'

'Not that I know of,' said Comrade Giles.

'Apparently, you can make it out of fertiliser,' suggested Comrade Brian, 'and we've got a shed-load of that!'

'Actually,' said Giles, 'we've got two shed-loads. We filled up Farmer Malcolm's in the spring.'

'And does anyone know how to make dynamite from fertiliser?' asked Florence.

Regrettably, nobody did.

Recalling the many days he'd spent studying Traffic Management during his Fast Track Graduate Police Training Programme, Inspector Capstan said, 'Maybe you could have a go at disrupting the island's flow of traffic instead?'

'What, like standing in front of it?' asked Flo.

'I was thinking more about swapping a few signposts around.'

'That's not a bad idea,' said Brian, Secretary of Vehicles and Recreation. 'If we took down all the one-way signs, painted over the double-yellow lines and replaced all the red traffic light bulbs with green ones, it would cause absolute chaos, and they'd probably just up sticks and leave simply to get as far away from the place as possible!'

As the members of the People's Independent Republic of the Isle of Wight's Resistance Movement smiled around at each other in agreement, Chairperson Florence looked at Inspector Capstan. 'I don't suppose you could stick around to help out a little? You really seem to know your stuff!'

Being paid a direct compliment was so rare in Capstan's line of work, that he was completely bowled over, and with hardly a second thought, said, 'I'd be delighted to.'

'Do you mind if I head back to the boat, Sir?' asked Dewbush. 'It's just that I don't know anything about sign posts or road markings, and so I doubt if I'd be of much use.'

'Don't worry, Sergeant. I can teach you. And besides, it's probably high-time you started to learn, don't you think?'

Chapter Thirty Four
A strong sense of camaraderie

16:59 BST

THE PEOPLE'S Independent Republic of the Isle of Wight's Town Hall, once home of the island's governing body, but now COCK's brand new headquarters, was an elegant 19th century Grade Two listed mansion, painted in brilliant white, located in the very heart of Ryde's busy town centre.

Sitting on a raised platform surrounded by a circle of stone steps that led up to its pillared entrance, it had an impressive, albeit oblique view of the Solent. Its position on the intersection between Melrose Street, Church Lane and Ryde's High Street made it the perfect place to organise and manage the many complexities of a modern day island society.

'I thought I asked for a Cornetto?' asked Morose, as Bazzer handed him a Viennartar instead, one of the new ones that was on a stick.

'I know, Gov. Sorry Gov, but it's all they 'ad.' He adjusted the position of a large machine gun that was slung over his shoulder to help make it more comfortable.

'And why's it taken you so bloody long? It's half-melted already.' To prevent the top of it from sliding off onto the carpet of the elegantly decadent ground

274

floor room that Morose had selected as being his new office, he gave it a salacious lick.

'It's the traffic, Gov. It's a fuck'n nightmare! The whole place is clogged up.'

Morose could clearly hear the noise of what sounded like a hundred cars parked bumper to bumper directly outside his office window, most of the owners of which must be permanently leaning on their horns.

He turned back to Bazzer. 'Were you at least able to pick up some pepperoni pizzas for tonight?'

'Er, no. Sorry again, Gov, but they didn't 'ave any left.'

'How about the ready meals and Nescafé Gold Blend I asked for?'

'Um. They'd run out of all that, and milk as well. The only thing they 'ad was Weetabix, but we couldn't see the point of buyin' that, not without hav'n milk to go with it.'

'You did go to the right sort of shop, didn't you? You know, the type that sells actual food?'

'We went to the big Safebusy's on the High Street, Gov, but the store manager guy said that they 'adn't 'ad their afternoon delivery, and with everyone panic-buying, they was runnin' out of just about everythin', Gov.'

'I hope, at least, you threatened him with physical violence?' asked Morose.

'Of course, Gov! That was the first thing we did. But it was obvious that he weren't lyin', as all the shelves was half-empty, like.'

'And where the fuck is everyone else?' asked Morose, realising that he hadn't seen any of the others since lunch time.

'Most of 'em are still out shopping for clothes, Gov, like you told 'em to.'

'Yes, but that was fucking hours ago. How long does it take to find a new pair of fucking jeans and a t-shirt?'

'There are still a couple on the roof though, Gov, keeping a lookout, like.'

As Morose continued to mull over why it was that a group of men needed quite so much time to steal some new clothes, there was a knock on the door and Bazzer's cousin, Gazzer, peered in.

'There's some local types 'ere to see you, Gov.'

'Just tell them to fuck off,' said Morose, whose primary reason for coming all the way to the Isle of Wight was to eat as many Cornettos as he damned well liked, and so was hardly in the best of moods.

'But they say that they're official representatives of the People's Independent Republic of the Isle of Wight's Resistance Movement, Gov, and they've got a white flag.'

'Are they armed?'

'Well, they've got some rakes, and a couple of shovels.'

'OK, they can come in, but they'll have to leave their gardening tools outside.'

'Right you are, Gov.' Opening the door wide, he turned round and called, 'Oi, you's lot! You can come in, but you gotta leave that gardening stuff out there.'

Bursting into the room came a well-proportioned woman with a round, freckled face, wearing wellies and a green bandana that was doing a poor job at controlling a mass of tangled grey hair. Behind her came five other people, including none other than Inspector Capstan and Sergeant Dewbush, dressed in their very own wellies, combat trousers, sports vests and khaki bandanas.

'I'm Florence Ruddy-Shelduck,' announced Flo, 'Chairperson of the People's Independent Republic of the Isle of Wight's Resistance Movement,' and without hardly a pause for breath, went on, 'I have here, in my hand, a petition signed by well over sixteen people, all demanding that you leave our island *immediately*!'

Ignoring the mad-looking woman, Morose had stopped eating his Viennartar mid-lick as he stared open-mouthed at Capstan and Dewbush with incomprehending disbelief.

Realising that Morose had seen straight through what he'd hoped to have been a substantial disguise, Capstan cleared his throat, narrowed his eyes and said, 'Hello, Morose!'

Behind him, Dewbush followed that up with, 'Hello, Sir!' adding, 'We've joined the People's Independent Republic of the Isle of Wight's Resistance Movement!' with all the excitement of a six year-old boy opening a generously-sized Christmas present to discover that he'd been given a PlayStation 4 bundled with Resident Evil 7: Biohazard.

Emerging from the shock of seeing his two former work colleagues, again, but this time dressed up as agricultural freedom fighters, Morose finally said, 'Inspector Cat Sperm and Sergeant Bush Poo. I just don't seem to be able to get rid of you!'

'So it would seem,' agreed Capstan, managing

something akin to a snarl.

Having spent a strenuous afternoon working side-by-side with their new brothers-in-arms, removing one-way signs, painting over double yellow lines, and replacing red traffic light bulbs with green ones, Capstan and Dewbush had gained a strong feeling of camaraderie for their fellow resistance fighters. And after seeing, first-hand, the results of all their hard work, which would probably best be described as island-infrastructural meltdown, they felt proud to have become a part of the People's Independent Republic of the Isle of Wight's Resistance Movement. So, when they'd all agreed that sufficient traffic chaos had been induced, they were only too keen to support their new leader, Chairperson Florence, in marching straight down to the Town Hall to hand-deliver their signed petition.

Having made it so far, and with renewed conviction of the difference between what was right and what was most definitely wrong, Capstan steadied himself on his stick and with the calm voice of authority said, 'Morose, we're here to escort you back to England to answer for your crimes against society and the British judicial system. Now, we don't want any trouble, so I suggest you come quietly.'

'Er, no, Capstan. I'm not going to come quietly. I'm not even going to come really noisily,' and with a glance over at Bazzer, he said, 'Shoot them, will you?'

Capstan gulped, and instinctively looked over at Dewbush for very possibly the last time, ever.

'What, all of them?' asked Bazzer, who'd been more used to killing people one at a time.

'No, just the ones in the middle,' replied Morose, with a thick layer of sarcasm.

'Right, Gov,' and Bazzer pointed his L7A2 GPMG belt-fed 7.62mm machine gun around at the different members of the resistance party, trying to decide which ones fell into the category of being in the middle.

Before he'd had a chance to make up his mind, a brief crackle of automatic gunfire echoed from somewhere off in the distance. Instinctively, they all stopped to listen, turning their heads towards the large bay window from where the sound had come, but all they could hear was the ongoing noise of horns being leant on and disgruntled drivers hurling abuse at each other. Just as Bazzer's brain returned to the task of working out which of those in front of him were more centralised than the others, they all heard the sound again, but much closer this time. The car owners outside must have heard it as well, as the noise of the horns and avid cursing dissipated to leave nothing but a quiet stillness, as if the whole of Ryde had stopped in its tracks in order to listen.

The sound of a huge explosion ripped through the air, directly outside the Town Hall, followed by the thud and ricochet of bullets as they bounced off the wall outside, and as everyone in the room dived for cover, Morose shouted, 'JESUS FUCKING CHRIST! WHAT THE FUCK IS GOING ON?' to anyone who happened to be listening.

But with everyone in the room fully focussed on trying to neither scream nor die, but with a fair representation of the island's shopping elite on the street outside finding themselves with little choice but to do both, one after the other, Morose shouted, 'BAZZER, GAZZER, GET OUTSIDE AND TELL ME WHAT THE FUCK IS HAPPENING OUT THERE!'

Another explosion lifted the ground beneath their feet, brought plaster from the ceiling above, and hurled a middle-aged male shopper straight through the Victorian bay window, to splatter against the far wall. With his beige shorts and blood-soaked white polo shirt, he looked remarkably like a sheep that had been casually discarded by a passing elephant who'd been using it as an organic, all-natural tampon. As everyone stared over at him, he began sliding down the wall to end up sitting at an unnatural angle on the floor, still clinging to a Safebusy's Forever bag advertising the half-price sale of Fair Trade Marijuana.

Bazzer turned to his boss and asked, 'Wot, out there, Gov?'

Another huge explosion erupted outside, this one right in the middle of the jammed up traffic, sending two cars into the air in a ball of flames and setting off just about every single car alarm within a hundred metre radius, the noise of which only added to the general melee.

With pragmatic consideration for the wellbeing of his bodyguards, Morose said, 'You'd better head up to the roof.'

As Capstan gave the former Safebusy customer another quick look, he suggested, 'It may be better if we *all* head up there!'

Everyone was in full agreement, even Morose, and

as bullets, and people, and cars, continued to fly around outside, with their heads kept as low to the ground as possible Bazzer and Gazzer led the party out into the Town Hall's lobby and up the sweeping Victorian staircase towards the top of the building, stopping only occasionally to duck behind the ornately decorated ironwork that supported its immaculately varnished solid oak hand rail.

Chapter Thirty Five
The battle just outside Burton's

16:59 BST

WITH A STRAIGHTFORWARD mooring of their fleet of nineteen VPLC Mk 5 Landing Craft on the beach at Ryde Esplanade, and weaving their way through endless numbers of jammed-up cars, the 56 Royal Marines Commando Unit made easy progress up Melrose Street towards the Town Hall at the top of the hill.

After inhaling their sample bags of *Cocainebelieve* back out on the Solent, a hundred yards out from Ryde Pier Head, all the men had felt remarkably upbeat. But Claire had taken her first sample a long time before that; exactly five and a half minutes after addressing the men, to be precise. Her performance on the stage, and the long journey down from MI6's headquarters, had left her completely drained of energy, and she was in dire need of a serious pick-me-up.

And it was probably because of the class A drug's effect on her mesolimbic dopamine system, combined with the rugged good looks of the unit's Commanding Officer, Lieutenant Colonel Frank Derwent, that shortly after the address she'd found herself persuading him to let her join them on the leading boat of the unit's landing party.

So there she was, kitted out in the smallest sized set of combat fatigues that they could dig out, her feet enclosed in a pair of size six heavy-duty army boots, and wearing the distinctive green beret that singled out the Royal Marines from other British armed forces. Obviously she hadn't done the requisite All Arms Commando Course needed to officially wear their beret, but it made her look dead cute, and as she'd effectively become their Ambassador, everyone was keen for her to wear it. The only thing she didn't have was a gun, for as happy as they were for her to dress up as one of them, giving her a 5.56mm Minimi Light Machine Gun without having been trained how to use it would have been unwise and, quite possibly, a little dangerous.

About three quarters of their way up to the top of Melrose Street, and with the Town Hall in their sights, they almost walked straight into a group of criminal insurgents as they ambled out of the Burton's menswear shop, carrying various shopping bags in one hand and their L7A2 GPMG belt-fed 7.62mm machine guns in the other.

Seeing them just in the nick of time, Frank grabbed Claire and dragged her behind the closest car, an old blue Volvo Estate that was stuck in the middle of the street along with all the others.

The insurgents stopped dead in their tracks and dropped their shopping bags to the pavement as they endeavoured to bring their machine guns level with their enemy. But the Royal Marines needed no such preparations to engage, and it only took one of them to take all three out with a single burst of rapid fire.

However, the noise had raised the alarm to others still inside the shop, and as they'd at least had a warning, unlike their criminal chums now lying dead outside the shop's frontage, they were able to ditch their bags and start shooting.

As a rain of 7.62mm bullets sprayed out from the shop's front, and the Royal Marines outside took cover, one of them had the foresight to lob a L109A1 HE Fragmentation Grenade in through the shop's wide open doors, giving those in the leading party the chance to advance past, before more shooting erupted from inside Burton's.

Forced to leave some of his men behind, Frank, Claire and a handful of others moved all the way up to the top of Melrose Street where they positioned themselves behind a variety of vehicles, about thirty metres from the stone steps that led up to the Town Hall's marble pillared entrance. Their arrival was met by more bullets, and without having a clue where they were coming from, Frank threw his own Fragmentation Grenade up towards the Town Hall's front doors, where it did exactly what it said it would do on the box that it came in, and exploded, forcing Frank to take shelter again.

It was then that a missile screeched down from the roof of the building to land directly between two other cars, only just missing them.

As all the car alarms were set off, and those shoppers still in one whole piece started to run for their very lives, a signal to Frank's men behind led them to focus their fire towards the top of the Town

Hall, where insurgents must have been hiding with some sort of hand-held missile system.

With the Royal Marines now shooting up, more bullets began to rain down on them from the same roof, pinning them behind the various vehicles that they were sheltering behind.

There Frank stayed, with Claire and the advanced party, waiting for the remainder of his unit to catch up, giving him valuable time to consider their next move.

Chapter Thirty Six
A defensive position

17:14 BST

FIRST TO ARRIVE on to the top of the Town Hall's roof was Bazzer, closely followed by his cousin, Gazzer, his boss, Morose, and then the various dignitaries forming the People's Independent Republic Party of the Isle of Wight's Resistance Movement, including Inspector Capstan, Sergeant Dewbush, Chairperson Flo, Comrade Giles, Comrade Jeffrey, and Comrade Brian. Unfortunately they weren't able to have brought Comrade John Long-Silverton with them, as much as they'd have liked to, as he was having a late afternoon nap back at their campsite.

Half-leaning out over the edge of the building ahead of them, staring down the telescopic sights of a couple of L7A2 GPMG belt-fed 7.62mm machine guns, were two members of the Criminal Organisation for Crime and Kidnapping, one with long greasy blonde hair and the other with shorter, dark brown hair. Being of average size, and having been that way when they were first arrested, they were the only two whose pre-prison clothes had still fitted them, so they'd been relatively happy to volunteer for roof-top lookout duty on the promise that they'd each get a Chocolate Chip Cornetto.

Staggering forward towards them, struggling desperately for air, Morose asked again, 'What the…fuck is…going on…down there?'

With neither turning round, the blonde haired one answered, 'Looks like the Royal Marines, Gov, judging by their berets.'

'Shit,' said Morose, who'd been kind of hoping it had been a handful of British police, dressed in riot gear. But this reminded him and he spun round, stared hard at Inspector Capstan, and said, 'Cat Spam, Bush Dew and the rest of you, I want you sitting down, over there,' and he pointed towards one of the rooftop's gutters where he thought would be a fitting place for them to hang around for a while.

'Bazzer, Gazzer, keep an eye on them. And if any of them move, shoot them!'

Morose then returned to the situation at hand: that of the advancing army.

'You know, it could be the SAS, Gov, and not the Royal Marines,' said the blonde-haired gunman.

'Don't you mean the SAABS?' suggested the other.

The blonde one looked over at the dark-haired one.

'Who the fuck are the SAABS?' he asked.

'It's what they called themselves, when they joined up with the Special Boat Service.'

'Bollocks!'

'It's true!'

'Nah. You're winding me up!'

'Swear to God!'

'Why'd they do that?'

'Government cutbacks, apparently.'

'So if it's not "Who dares, wins", and all that

anymore, then what is it?'

'They changed it to "Who dares, swims,"

'Fuck off!'

'Anyway, it's not them. It's gotta be the Royal Marines. There's too many of them to be Special Forces. They must've come up from the beach, down by the esplanade.'

'WILL YOU TWO SHUT THE FUCK UP!' shouted Morose, who'd managed to regain control of his breathing, a little, and had crouched down behind the low wall that surrounded the top of the building.

With a high degree of caution he peered over the side.

Moving between the rows of recently abandoned cars, some of which were still burning but all of which seemed to still be under the mistaken belief that someone was trying to steal them, he could see dozens upon dozens of soldiers making their way up Melrose street towards the Town Hall, each one taking a defensive position behind a car once they were in about a thirty metre radius of the stone steps.

'We would fire another missile at them, Gov, but we only had one,' offered the blonde criminal insurgent crouched nearest to Morose.

'And how are you doing for ammo?' asked Morose.

'Er, not great, Gov. We had two belts each, and we're both on the last one already.'

'Shit,' said Morose, again, as he too reflected on what to do next.

Chapter Thirty Seven
A lull in the fire

17:23 BST

WITH WHAT LOOKED to be the bulk of his unit making their way up to their advanced position outside the Town Hall, Lieutenant Colonel Frank Derwent peered through the rear door windows of a red Vauxhall Astra, and stared up towards the Town Hall's main entrance. He couldn't see any movement coming from behind the marble pillars, but there were people inside, possibly a group of insurgents, moving into position within the shadows of the lobby.

The concentration of fire was still coming from the roof. He couldn't see anything coming from any other part of the building, and he certainly couldn't hear much, not over the car alarms, roof-top gunfire and screaming shoppers. But the fact that he could neither see nor hear anything else, from anywhere else, except what he'd glimpsed inside the entrance hall didn't mean much. The Grade Two listed 19th century mansion had dozens of windows, and with the glare of the summer sun against its painted white walls, they were all just ominous dark shadows, each of which could easily disguise a sniper, or simply an insurgent with another missile.

'What's the plan?' asked Claire, crouching down beside him with the look of a lioness, out on the hunt.

'The plan is that you keep your head down, young lady! I should never have allowed you to come with us, and if I'd have known they'd have advanced military weapons, like hand-held missile systems and the like, I wouldn't have!'

But Claire felt empowered, energized, and alive; and it wasn't just the cocaine. For possibly the first time in her life, as she dodged bullets behind an old Astra in the middle of what had been called the Isle of Wight, she had a sense of place, of belonging, of purpose, and the screaming bullets and shoppers doing something similar, had only seemed to act as a catalyst for her heightened emotional state.

But realising that there had been a lull in the fire, and itching to get up to start actually doing something, she said, 'Well, I suggest we just attack them, head-on!' and without warning, grabbed the machine gun out of Frank's hands, leapt up and launched herself over the bonnet of the Astra to pelt out onto the street, heading fast for the stone steps.

'Jesus fucking Christ,' said Frank, and drawing his pistol out from its holster, bellowed to his men, '*FORWARD!!!*' as he too jumped up from his defensive position to follow her, shooting madly up at the roof as he hurled himself towards the Town Hall's entrance, hoping to God that his men would follow, and that those on the roof weren't just waiting for such a golden opportunity to blow them into an alternative reality.

Chapter Thirty Eight
Fight them off for as long as you can

17:28 BST

'THERE'S A GIRL down there!' said the long-haired blonde criminal insurgent.

'Uh-huh,' said the other, with only passing interest as he was trying really hard to count how many rounds he had left.

'She just jumped over the bonnet of that there red car,' continued the insurgent as he watched her through his gun's telescopic sights. 'And she's runnin', quick as fuck, towards them steps, like!'

'Is that so?'

'She's fuck'n fit too!'

'Let's 'ave a look.' Having been unable to get past ten without losing count, the dark-haired criminal insurgent gave up and peered down at her.

'Blimey! She's a right fuck'n corker!'

Morose had also seen her, but with other things on his mind other than ogling at some soldier-girl, even a remarkably attractive one, asked, 'As she looks just like all the other members of the British armed forces down there, being that she's got a gun and everything, I don't suppose there's any chance that one of you could make some sort of an effort to *shoot her*? Or is that asking too much?'

'You mean, you wan' us to shoot a - a...*girl?*' asked the dark-haired one, as he and the blonde guy turned to stare at their boss with an expression of undisguised incredulity.

'Well, look,' continued Morose, in a conversational tone, 'if you're not going to kill the girl, then I don't suppose it's at all possible that you could spare a moment to shoot at the other hundred or so British soldiers who are, as I speak, *storming the FUCKING BUILDING?*'

It was the gunmen's turn to say, 'Shit', as they simultaneously turned to continue with the job at hand; that of defending their headquarters against what had quickly become an all-out, full-frontal assault by either the Royal Marines, the SAS, the SBS, the SAABS, or a subtle combination of all four.

But it had become clear from Morose's perspective that they were out-gunned and out-numbered, and despite the fact that he'd managed to acquire another interesting assortment of hostages, two of whom were the same he'd tried using before, the time for attempting to negotiate some sort of a deal had long gone.

So he made his way to the back of the building and peered over the edge, looking for a fire escape, or something that he could use to make a swift but much needed exit. But all he could see were a couple of drainpipes, and there was no way he was going to be able to shimmy down them, not unless he was able to discover some brand new diet that could shed at least a hundred kilograms in about two and a half minutes. So he stared down at the garden patio beneath and said,

'Oi, Bazzer, Gazzer, come over 'ere!'

As his two bodyguards lumbered towards him, Morose asked, 'Can you see that down there?'

'What's that, Gov?' asked Bazzer, glancing over the edge.

'Look, it's there. Can't you see it?'

As they both leaned further out in an effort to see whatever it was that their boss was asking them to look at, Bazzer said, 'I can't see noffin', Gov. Just a patio.'

Morose surreptitiously stepped behind them.

'You just need to get closer,' he said, adding, 'Like this!' and gave them both a really hard shove.

'What the fuuuuuuu..?' said either Bazzer, or Gazzer, but it was difficult to tell which, as they'd already begun a very rapid descent of the Town Hall to land, splatted out, on the patio beneath.

Morose leaned over the side to check that they'd ended up as he'd hoped, like a couple of makeshift mattresses to help break his own fall.

And with the sound of gunfire, explosions, shouting, and doors being opened and closed getting closer by the second, he felt the time had nearly arrived for him to make his own departure, but he still had one more job to do.

Glancing over at Capstan and Dewbush, still huddled together with their agricultural freedom fighting chums, he called over to the last two remaining members of his criminal fighting force.

'I don't suppose I could borrow one of your guns for a moment, could I?'

'We're nearly out've ammo anyways, Gov,' said the

blonde one. And as he'd run out of soldiers to shoot at as well, due to the fact that the vast majority of them had made it safely into the building, he pushed himself up from the ground, stretched out his back and handed Morose his machine gun.

'Thanks,' said Morose, and as he turned back towards the group huddled in the corner, who all stared back at him like a herd of bunnies trapped by approaching headlights during a night-time excursion to the central reservation of the M42, said, 'Fight them off for as long as you can, lads. I'm going to take care of this lot.'

'But what about me, Gov?' asked the blonde one. 'You've got me gun!'

'Well, you'll just have to improvise, won't you?'

'Right you are, Gov.'

As the two men ducked back through the roof's door, ready for one of them, at least, to shoot anyone coming up the other way, Morose was able to give his former subordinates, and those with them, his full and undivided attention.

'So, Cat's Bum and Bush Spew. Here we are, once again!'

The two policemen attempted to stare back at Morose with dignified contempt, but probably looked more like a couple of people just hanging around, waiting to be executed. Capstan desperately thought back to the time of his Fast Track Graduate Police Training Programme, to see if he could remember something, anything, he may have been taught to help extricate himself from what looked to be certain death. And with just a glimmer of hope, asked, 'I hope you're not planning on doing anything silly with that machine gun you've got there?'

Sergeant Dewbush, Chairperson Florence and the other members of the resistance delegation all shook their heads, hoping that by doing so, this demented, fat, bald, psychotic machine gun-wielding nut-job standing in front of them, wouldn't.

'How d'you mean?' asked Morose, who must have either forgotten about the day when he, himself, had been taught to use the old "I hope you're not going to do anything silly with that" ploy, or had missed the lesson due to ill health.

'Well, you know. Like shoot us, or something,' said Capstan, before remembering to add the line, 'You'd only be making it worse for yourself!'

Instead of shaking their heads, Dewbush, Florence and the other members of the resistance delegation now all started to nod, and with some vigour. They were in full and unequivocal agreement.

'I see,' said Morose. 'So, if I *was* to shoot you in the leg, for example, like this,' and he fired a single round into the middle of Capstan's thigh.

'*ARRRGGGHHH…FUCK!*' screamed Capstan, grabbing what had been his dodgy leg, but was now probably going to have to be replaced with something more mechanical, and useful. '*You fat, fucking, fucked-up, fucking miserable fucking bastard!*'

'As I was saying,' continued Morose. 'If I was to shoot either one of you in the leg, like this,' and he fired again, but this time into his intellectually-challenged former Sergeant.

'*OWWWWW!*' shouted Dewbush, clutching at his

own leg. '*THAT REALLY HURT!*'

'Then I'm only making it worse for myself?' continued Morose, with a quizzical look. 'Is that what you meant?'

But with pure white-hot pain tearing its way along Capstan's thigh, the best response he could come up with was, '*That's right!*'

And as Morose was about to ask Capstan exactly *how* shooting them in either the leg, arm, chest or head, would be "only making it worse for himself", he heard a prolonged burst of automatic gunfire coming from the stairwell.

It really was time for him to go!

'Look, chaps,' he said. 'I'd love to stay and chat, but unfortunately I need to be off,' and aimed his gun directly at Capstan's head.

And as Capstan held out his hand, hoping, praying that by some miracle he could be blessed with superhuman powers, enabling the palm of his hand to deflect the bullet fired out of a L7A2 GPMG belt-fed 7.62mm machine gun, Morose pulled the trigger.

'Crap!'

He'd run out of bullets.

And judging by the noise coming from the stairwell, time as well.

'It must be your lucky day,' he said, and hurling the now useless gun at Capstan's head, made his way over to the back of the building.

But with his hand still held up to protect himself from being shot, the machine gun just bounced off Capstan's arm to fall relatively harmlessly in his lap.

When Morose reached the low wall, he glanced

over the edge to make sure his two bodyguards were still where they were supposed to be, ready and waiting to do their job for the very last time. They were, of course, so he climbed onto it, and sat there for a moment as he psyched himself up, ready for the jump. And just before he pushed himself off, he glanced back at Capstan, who was clearly struggling to maintain consciousness.

'Until next time, Cat Spam,' and with that, and a broad fat grin, he disappeared over the side.

Chapter Thirty Nine
An angel wearing mascara

17:45 BST

CAPSTAN COULD feel himself drifting into what felt like an ocean of memories. With the amount of blood he'd seen pulsing out of his leg, he could only assume that Morose's bullet must have severed his femoral artery. But he'd been determined not to bleed out before watching his former boss, Chief Inspector Morose of the Solent Police, the man found guilty of being the Psychotic Serial Slasher of Southampton and the South Coast, and the very man who'd since become the Head of COCK, the Centre for Organised Crime and Kidnapping, jump off the roof of the building.

But Morose had gone now, and with any luck, had landed on his feet, breaking both his legs in the process, the force of which may have been enough to rupture his spleen and induce a massive cardiac arrest.

And with that comforting, albeit unlikely thought, he began to let himself drift away.

As his eyelids flickered, he heard another burst of automatic gunfire. But then he knew he was very nearly gone, because a beautiful heavenly angel appeared before his eyes, wearing a green beret and a fair amount of mascara.

'I'm Claire Bridlestock,' the angel told him, 'the Prime Minister's Marketing & Public Relations Consultant.'

But she didn't look anything like a Marketing & Public Relations Consultant, for the Prime Minister or anyone else. More like a Page 3 model on her way to her next military-themed photoshoot.

And that was when he realised that he must be dreaming. And as the gorgeous heavenly being placed her hand on his injured leg and turned to scream, *'MEDIC! MEDIC! WILL SOMEONE PLEASE GET A FUCKING MEDIC!'* Detective Inspector Capstan, formally of Bath City Police, but more recently of the Solent Constabulary, and the holder of an OBE along with two Queen's Police Medals for Gallantry and Distinguished Service, slipped, not very peacefully, into what he hoped would be a deep, untroubled sleep, but which could have just as easily been the end of both his life, and subsequently his illustrious career as a British policeman.

And as he tried to make what could very well have been his last ever conscious thoughts to be about his wife and children, or even the angel still before his eyes, who he just realised had suspiciously dilated pupils, all he could actually think about was his subordinate, Sergeant bloody Dewbush, and if he was ever going to settle down, pass his driving test, and find that dog he was looking for. *What was its name?* Capstan thought. *Oh yes, that's right, Pencil Case. What sort of a complete moron would be stupid enough to call a bloody dog after an inanimate object designed primarily to keep felt-tip pens in?*

Claire's thoughts, meanwhile, were becoming more maternal by the second as she watched the French-looking man in front of her visibly sag as his head rolled forward to rest against his chest, like a shagged-out commuter returning late one night from the office Christmas party.

'MEDIC!' she screamed again. She'd no idea if he was dead or alive, but he certainly didn't look very well, and she pressed her hand down more firmly against his wounded thigh.

It was only then that she recognised Chairperson Florence, and the other members of the Peoples' Independent Republic of the Isle of Wight.

'Are you all OK?' she asked them.

'We're fine, my dear,' answered Florence. 'I didn't know you were a Royal Marine?'

Claire glanced down at her uniform, and then back up at her. 'Just for today, but it has been fun!'

'Excuse me?' said a younger looking man sitting alongside the guy who'd passed out, raising his hand as he did so, 'But I've been shot as well, you know.'

'I'll be with you in just a moment,' answered Claire, who'd taken hold of the French looking chap's wrist, searching for a pulse.

'And it really hurts!' added the man.

A Royal Marine crouched down beside Claire, digging out a field dressing and a pair of scissors from his back pack as he did so.

'I'll take over from here, miss,' he said, and as he knelt down beside the man whose head still lay on his chest, Claire turned her attention back to the other one.

'Now, where did you say you'd been shot?'

With a broad grin he answered, 'It's my leg, miss. If you put your hand here, you'll feel it.'

Placing her hand on the very upper part of his thigh, Claire could feel something, but it wasn't his leg. She looked at him as he continued to smile at her and said, 'You seem to be absolutely fine.'

'Thanks miss, but it's still sore. If you could keep it there for just a little longer, I'd really appreciate it.'

He was quite cute, so she obliged, and as she did so her mobile began to ring.

Digging it out with her free hand she answered, 'Hello?'

'Claire, it's me. How's it all going?'

It was her uncle, Robert Bridlestock, the British Prime Minister.

'Oh, fine. We've re-taken the Town Hall at Ryde, and are just tidying up,' and she gave the young man whose thigh she'd now started to gently massage a flirtatious smile. He was almost attractive, in a peculiar sort of a way.

'Splendid, Claire, splendid! You really have saved the day. The Evening Standard's just come out and its headline reads, "PM turns tide for Isle of Wight!" And they've even used a picture we sent them of me, standing in a puddle, wearing wellies and kissing a baby, which we think looks just great.'

'I'm delighted for you, Uncle, but when I get back we're going to have to sit down and re-negotiate my salary. I mean, I don't mind risking life and limb for Queen and Country, and all that, but I at least expect to get paid something half-decent!'

'Okay, but don't be too long,' said Robert. 'Freddy's managed to dig out a bottle of British wine that I thought we could drink to celebrate.'

'What's it called?' asked Claire, with some reservation.

'Er, let's see. Here it is. *Dorking Rouge Avec Des Raisins.*'

'That still sounds French, Uncle.'

'No, it's definitely British. It says so on the back.'

'Okay, but just because you've managed to find a wine that was actually produced in Britain, still doesn't validate your decision to leave the EU!'

'You're not still going on about that?'

'Yes, I am still going on about that!'

'I forgot to ask,' said Robert, in a bid to change the subject, 'but I don't suppose you could pick up some duty free marijuana whilst you're there?'

'How much do you want?'

'Oh, I don't know. A couple of sacks? Three, perhaps?'

'I'll see what I can do, Uncle, but I'm going to have to go now. I'm dealing with a seriously injured young man here, and he's just given me his phone number.'

ABOUT THE AUTHOR

B ORN in a US Navy hospital in California, David spent the first eight years of his life being transported from one country to another, before ending up in a three bedroom semi-detached house in Devon, on the South Coast of England.

David's father, a devout Navy Commander, and his Mother, a loyal Christian missionary, then decided to pack him off to an all-boys boarding school in Surrey, where they thought it would be fun for him to take up ballet. Once there, he showed a remarkable aptitude for dance and, being the only boy in the school to learn, found numerous opportunities to demonstrate the many and varied movements he'd been taught, normally whilst fending off attacks from his classroom chums who seemed unable to appreciate the skill required to turn around in circles, without falling over.

Meanwhile, his father began to push him down the more regimented path towards becoming a trained assassin, and spent the school holidays teaching him how to use an air rifle. Over the years, and with his father's expert tuition, he became a proficient marksman, managing to shoot a number of things directly in the head. His most common targets were birds but also extended to those less obvious, including his brother, sister, an uncle who popped in for tea, and several un-suspecting neighbours caught doing some gardening.

Horrified by the prospect of her youngest son spending his adult life travelling the world to indiscriminately kill people, for no particular reason, his mother intensified her efforts for him to enter the more highbrow world of the theatre by applying him to enter for the Royal Ballet. But after his twenty minute audition, during which time he jumped and twirled just as high and as fast as he possibly could, the three ballet aficionados who'd stared at him throughout with unhidden incredulity, proclaimed to his proud mother that the best and only role they could offer him would be that of, "Third Tree from the Left" during their next performance of Pinocchio, but that would involve him being cut down, with an axe, during the opening scene. Furthermore, they'd be unable to guarantee his safety as the director had decided to use a real axe instead of the normal foam rubber one, to add to the drama of an otherwise rather staid production.

A few weeks later, and unable to find any suitable life insurance, David's mother gave up her dream for him to become a famed Primo Ballerino and left him to his own devices.

And so it was, that with a sense of freedom little before known, he enrolled himself at a local college to study Chain Smoking, Under-Age Drinking, Drug Abuse and Fornication but forgot all about his core academic subjects. Subsequently he failed his 'A' Levels and moved to live in a tent in Dorking where he picked up with his more practised skills whilst working as a Barbed Wire Fencer.

Having being able to survive the hurricane of '87, the one that took down every tree within a fifty mile radius of his tent, he felt blessed, and must have been destined for greater things, other than sleeping rough during the night and being repeatedly stabbed by hard to control pieces of metal during the day. So he talked his way onto a Business Degree Course at the University of Southampton.

After three years of intensive study and to the surprise of just about everyone, he graduated with a 2:1 and spent the next ten years working in several incomprehensibly depressing sales jobs in Central London, before setting up his own recruitment firm.

Seven highly profitable years later, during which time he married and had two children, the Credit Crunch hit, which ended that particular episode of his career.

It's at this point he decided to become a writer which is where you find him now, happily married and living in London with his young family.

When not writing he spends his time attempting to persuade his wife that she really doesn't need to buy the entire contents of Ikea, even if there is a sale on. And when there are no items of flat-packed furniture for him to assemble he enjoys writing, base-jumping, and drawing up plans to demolish his house to build the world's largest charity shop.

www.david-blake.com

Printed in Great Britain
by Amazon